teach yourself®

sage line 50

mac bride

teach yourself

sage line 50

mac bride

for over 60 years, more than 40 million people have learnt over 750 subjects the **teach yourself** way, with impressive results.

be where you want to be with **teach yourself**

For UK order enquiries: please contact Bookpoint Ltd, 130 Milton Park, Abingdon, Oxon OX14 4SB. Telephone: +44 (0)1235 827720. Fax: +44 (0)1235 400454. Lines are open 09.00–18.00, Monday to Saturday, with a 24-hour message answering service. Details about our titles and how to order are available at www.teachyourself.co.uk.

For USA order enquiries: please contact McGraw-Hill Customer Services, PO Box 545, Blacklick, OH 43004-0545, USA. Telephone: 1-800-722-4726. Fax: 1-614-755-5645.

For Canada order enquiries: please contact McGraw-Hill Ryerson Ltd, 300 Water St, Whitby, Ontario L1N 9B6, Canada. Telephone: 905 430 5000. Fax: 905 430 5020.

Long renowned as the authoritative source for self-guided learning – with more than 40 million copies sold worldwide – the **teach yourself** series includes over 300 titles in the fields of languages, crafts, hobbies, business, computing and education.

British Library Cataloguing in Publication Data: a catalogue record for this title is available from The British Library.

Library of Congress Catalog Card Number: on file.

First published in UK 2006 by Hodder Education, 338 Euston Road, London, NW1 3BH.

First published in US 2006 by Contemporary Books, a Division of the McGraw-Hill Companies, 1 Prudential Plaza, 130 East Randolph Street, Chicago, IL 60601, USA.

The **teach yourself** name is a registered trademark of Hodder Headline.

Typeset by MacDesign, Southampton

Printed in Great Britain for Hodder Education, a division of Hodder Headline, 338 Euston Road, London NW1 3BH, by Cox & Wyman Ltd, Reading, Berkshire.

Hodder Headline's policy is to use papers that are natural, renewable and recyclable products and made from wood grown in sustainable forests. The logging and manufacturing processes are expected to conform to the environmental regulations of the country of origin.

Impression number   10 9 8 7 6 5 4 3 2

Year   2010 2009 2008 2007 2006

v

contents

preface

Sage is the UK's leading accountancy software house, and its central product, Line 50, is the UK's most widely-used accounts system – or rather set of systems. Line 50 comes in three sizes: Accountant, Accountant Plus and Financial Controller. All share a common core, but the latter two have extra features that larger businesses may need – and you can move your data from one to the next as your business grows. (And if it gets really big, Line 100 and Line 200 are there for you!)

The software follows the standard double-entry, three-ledger approach to bookkeeping, but with the addition of a whole range of analysis, reporting and other management information tools, plus the normal time- and effort-saving facilities that you would expect from any good computerized system. This combination of simplicity and comprehensive coverage, plus the tried and tested reliability of the software, are why Sage systems are so widely used.

Chapter 1 provides a brief introduction to the accountancy principles behind the software – because if you understand how a system works and why things are done the way they are, you will master it more quickly and be more able to sort out problems later. The rest of the book demonstrates how to use the various modules and facilities, for day-to-day accounting, for the end of period summaries and reports, and for analysis at any time. I have not tried to cover every aspect of the software – there's a manual for that – but instead have concentrated on the essentials, in the hope that this will help to build a firm foundation of understanding and the confidence to tackle the minor features, if you need to use them.

Mac Bride
Southampton, 2006

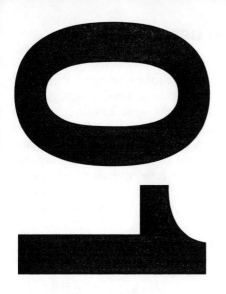

the principles of accounts

In this chapter you will learn:

- why businesses need to keep accounts
- about double-entry bookkeeping and the three-ledger system
- about the trial balance, profit and loss account and balance sheet

1.1 The common basis

Though businesses vary enormously in what they do and how they do it, large parts of their accounting systems are essentially the same. An electrician, a violin-maker, a web design partnership, a clothes manufacturer, a chain store and the chap who runs the corner-shop may not seem to have much in common. They deal in different products and services; some employ many people, others work alone; some have many over-the-counter customers, some work for a few carefully-cultivated clients; some deal almost entirely in cash, others trade on credit with their customers and suppliers. Despite this, the basic structures and operations of their accounts are the same.

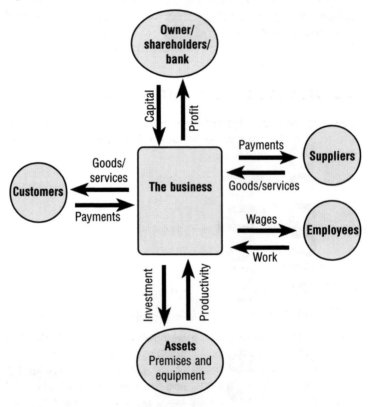

The common structure ... and the flow of money, goods and services between the components. (Taxes have been omitted for the sake of clarity.)

Every business has:

- **Customers,** to whom they supply goods or services.

- **Suppliers** of goods and services – from accountancy to Yellow Pages ads. A manufacturing business will also have suppliers of raw materials.

- **Owner(s)** – a sole trader, a group of partners or the shareholders of a company.

- **Assets** – premises, vehicles, machinery, office furniture and equipment.

The business may also have **employees.** The standard Line 50 accounts software handles wages, tax and National Insurance as business expenses, but does not cover employees' individual work records and wage slips. If you are interested, Sage produce Payroll software that is compatible with Line 50.

1.2 Accounts and information

The purpose of any accounting system is to record transactions and to provide information about the business. It must be able to tell you such things as:

- The amounts you owe to suppliers.

- The amounts owed to you by customers.

- The total sales and purchases during a period.

- The expenses incurred in running the business, e.g. rent, power, stationery, salaries.

- The value of cash in hand and at the bank.

- The value of the business's capital assets.

Most of these amounts and values have to be calculated, and with a manual system, that takes time. With the Sage systems, as with all good accounts software, the calculations are done for you. Most of these totals and values are automatically brought up to date as each new transaction is posted; others are updated during end-of-year routines.

The software can also produce, at a click of a button, a range of financial statements and summaries – of which all can be useful and some are essential. These include:

- A **profit and loss (P & L) account** to show the overall trading position. Is the business making a profit? And how much?

- A **balance sheet** showing the assets and liabilities.

- **Departmental analyses** of profit and loss.

- **Summaries** and **graphs** showing the patterns of trade with individual customers and suppliers.

- **VAT returns**.

1.3 Double-entry bookkeeping

Double-entry bookkeeping is the basis of all modern accounting systems. It works like this.

A separate *account* – a record of transactions – is kept for each customer and supplier, for each category of expenses, assets and debts, for each bank account, etc.

It is called double-entry bookkeeping because every transaction is recorded twice – as a *debit* in one account and as a *credit* in another. When an item is purchased, its value is added to the appropriate expense or stock account, and the same amount removed from a cash, bank or supplier's account.

Bank Account			
Debit	**£**	**Credit**	**£**
		Purchases	690

Purchases Account			
Debit	**£**	**Credit**	**£**
300 widgets (bank)	690		

- A **debit** is the movement of value into an account – e.g. when goods are purchased, this is a debit in the stock account.

- A **credit** is the movement of value out of an account, e.g. the money to pay for purchases will come from the bank or cash account, and be recorded as a credit there.

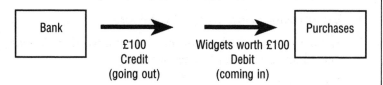

Because the movement of money into one account is always balanced by an outward movement from another, the totals of the credits and debits should always be the same. A Trial Balance (page 13), which compares those totals, provides a first-level check of the accuracy of the accounts.

Credit = out debit = in

Newcomers to accounts can sometimes be confused over debit and credit – when you are working with some accounts the use of 'credit' or 'debit' to describe a transaction seems a bit counter-intuitive. The 'real world' use of the terms is much slacker than their use in accounting. Stick to the golden rule: it's a credit when the value is being moved out of the account, and a debit to the account that the value is being moved into.

Assets and liabilities

An **asset** is something which can be turned into cash, so either something that we own, or money that is owed to us. Assets are divided into two categories:

- **Fixed assets**: those have more or less constant value, such as buildings, equipment, furnishings and vehicles.

- **Current assets**: those which fluctuate during the course of the year as the business trades, such as stock, cash in the bank and monies owed by customers.

When assets are acquired they are recorded as debit entries in their accounts, with balancing credit entries elsewhere. With purchases of stock and fixed assets, the credit entries will probably be in the bank account. (This 'Bank Account' is your record of cheques paid and received. It is not the same as the account held at the bank, though they should tally.) Where the asset is money owed the credit entry goes in a special control account.

Liabilities are the amounts owed by the business. They are also divided into two categories:

♦ **Capital:** money invested by the owners (either personally or as shareholders), profits ploughed back into the firm, bank loans and other long-term debts. These may appear in the accounts under the heading '**Financed By**'.

♦ **Current liabilities:** debts which change during trading – money owed in taxes or to suppliers, bank overdrafts.

Capital

The term is used loosely to mean several slightly different things. When a business is first started, 'capital' refers to the money put into it to get things going. A loan is sometimes referred to as 'working capital', though strictly speaking this means the difference between current assets and current liabilities. In an ongoing business, capital can be defined as the excess of assets over liabilities – the value of the business if all its assets are sold and debts paid.

Example: The start-up

Smith and Jones pool their savings to start a business. They begin by buying a machine to make widgets and a van to deliver them. Here are the key accounts after the initial setting up. These are hugely simplified! Transactions would normally be recorded in far more detail – at the very least they should have the date and an invoice or other reference number. There should a clear 'audit trail' – a simple way to trace the flow of money through the business.

Capital Account			
Debit	**£**	**Credit**	**£**
		Smith (Bank)	10,000
		Jones (Bank)	10,000
		Balance	20,000

Vehicles Account			
Debit	**£**	**Credit**	**£**
Van (Bank)	8,000		
Balance	8,000		

Equipment Account			
Debit	**£**	**Credit**	**£**
Machine (Bank)	4,000		
Balance	4,000		

Bank Account			
Debit	**£**	**Credit**	**£**
Smith (Capital)	10,000		
Jones (Capital)	10,000		
	20,000	Van (Vehicles)	8,000
		Machine (Equip't)	4,000
			12,000
Balance 20,000 – 12,000 = 8,000			

Each account has been totalled to give its current balance. As the Bank account has both debit and credit entries, both sides have been totalled and the balance is the difference between the two. Add up debit and credit balances and you get the same £20,000 total.

1.4 Customers and Suppliers

In a paper-based system, the individual accounts are held in *books of account*, or *ledgers* – the *Sales*, *Purchase* and *Nominal ledgers*. The Sage system follows this convention, but refers to the Sales ledger as the *Customers* navigation group or module, and the Purchase ledger as the *Suppliers* module.

The Sales ledger (Customers)

If customers buy from you on credit, they will each have their own separate account, where you record the date and value of each sale and of each payment made. With Sage software, not only can you easily see which payments are outstanding – and for how long – you can just as easily generate reminder letters to the slower-paying debtors. There are also a report generator, a Graph facility and other tools to enable you to analyse and understand the patterns and trends of your trading with any one or more selected customers.

The Sales ledger is a collection of customers' accounts. There will be one or more other accounts – in the Nominal ledger – which keep track of sales overall. A small firm might just have one general Sales account; a larger one is more likely to have Sales accounts for each area of the firm's business.

Cash, not credit

Over-the-counter cash sales would normally be recorded directly into the Sales (and Bank) accounts. Similarly, anything bought for cash would be recorded in the appropriate expenses and purchases acounts.

If you do have purely cash dealings with any customer or suppliers, it may be worth setting up individual accounts for them if you want to monitor your trade with them. One of the reasons for keeping accounts is to collect information which you can use to improve your business. Understanding your trading patterns always helps.

The Purchase ledger (Suppliers)

This is the mirror image of the Sales ledger, recording the details of your dealings – on credit – with your suppliers. Each entry will be matched by a balancing entry in the Nominal ledger, where there will be accounts for purchases of stock and raw materials, and other expenses. (NB: in accountancy, *purchases* refers only to raw materials and goods bought for resale; all other costs are *expenses*.)

1.5 The Nominal ledger

This is the heart of a manual system – if you had no credit sales or purchases, it is the only one you would need. All accounts, except those for credit customers and suppliers, are stored here.

The Nominal ledger in Line 50

In the Sage system, the Nominal ledger accounts are accessed through two modules or navigation groups. The bank and cash accounts, and their associated activities are in the Bank group. The whole ledger, including the bank accounts, with the tools for analysing the finances, and handling end-of-period routines, VAT returns, etc. are in the Company group.

Exactly how you organize your nominal accounts is up to you – they should reflect the realities of your business. As a general rule, you set up an account for each aspect of the money flow that you want to be able to monitor. For example, in a small business, where the office expenses only add up to a few hundred a year, one account would be adequate to record them all. In a larger firm, separate accounts for paper, postage, cleaning, electricity, coffee, etc. would enable managers to see clearly how and when money was being spent – and therefore to forecast future spending, and perhaps find some savings.

Some accounts are essential. You must have ones for:

- Capital and long-term loans
- Fixed assets

- Cash in hand and at the bank
- Sales of goods and services
- Expenses.

Retailing or manufacturing businesses also need accounts for:

- Purchases of goods and materials, and current stock
- Labour, advertising and other expenses directly related to producing and selling goods.

The Nominal ledger in Line 50

The Sage system comes with a comprehensive set of Nominal accounts. We will look later (page 81) at how to adapt or add to these to suit your business; for the moment just notice the way they are organized.

Each account has a reference number, or *nominal code*, with the numbering set so that related ones are close together. When summaries are being prepared, groups of accounts can be totalled simply by setting ranges. For example, the first four are:

0010	Freehold Property
0011	Leasehold Property
0012	Land
0020	Plant and Machinery

The total of the range 0010 to 0012 is the value of all property and land. If you wanted to create accounts for more categories of property or land, by numbering them 0013, 0014, etc., you only need to extend the range to get a summary property value.

A little further down the list you will find

0030	Office Equipment
0040	Furniture and Fixtures
0050	Motor Vehicles

Setting the range 0010 to 0050 will therefore give the value of all fixed assets.

This pattern runs right through the system, with groups of accounts separated from the next by breaks in the number sequence.

The Nominal structure

Fixed assets

0 – Premises, etc.

Current Assets

1000 – Stock

1100 – Debtors

1200 – Bank

Current Liabilities

2100 – Creditors

2200 – Tax Control

2300 – Loans

Capital & Reserves

3000 – Share capital

3200 – Profit & Loss

Income

4000 – Work done

4200 – Sales of assets

4900 – Other income

Purchases

5000 – Materials

5200 – Stock

Direct Expenses

6000 – Labour

6200 – Advertising

Overheads

7000 – Wages & Salaries

7100 – Premises' costs

7200 – Expenses

8000 – Depreciation

Trouble-shooting

9998 – Suspense A/c

9999 – Mispostings

An outline of the Nominal ledger structure in Sage Line 50

1.6 Analysis and outputs

The accounts themselves are simply records of transactions, but the accounting system is more than that. It is also a means of assessing the health of the business and analysing its performance. There are three key outputs from any manual system, and they are all present – along with many others – in Sage Line 50. And, of course, the big difference between a manual system and Sage, is that with Sage you get the outputs at the touch of a

---

Bridge Computers
Period Trial Balance

N/C	Name	Debit £	Credit £
0020	Plant and Machinery	18,000.00	
0030	Office Equipment	5,400.00	
0040	Furniture and Fixtures	1,240.00	
0050	Motor Vehicles	11,410.00	
1001	Stock	11,800.00	
1100	Debtors Control Account	7,743.27	
1200	Bank Current Account	1,623.30	
1230	Petty Cash	1,200.00	
2100	Creditors Control Account		10,879.75
2200	Sales Tax Control Account		1,153.27
2201	Purchase Tax Control Account	1,068.45	
3001	Owners' Investment		20,000.00
4000	Computer systems		45,680.00
4001	Peripherals and parts		56,960.00
4002	Software packages		49,197.00
5000	Materials Purchased	62,320.00	
6201	Advertising	1,500.00	
7001	Directors' Salaries	24,000.00	
7004	Wages	29,950.00	
7100	Rent	2,105.00	
7103	General Rates	1,010.00	
7200	Electricity	2,000.00	
7502	Telephone	1,500.00	
	Totals:	183,870.02	183,870.02

button, instead of having to spend hours, or even days, with a pencil, paper and calculator. The key outputs are the trial balance, the profit and loss account and the balance sheet.

The trial balance

The trial balance shows the current debit and credit balance on each account, and the total of all debits and credits.

In a manual accounting system, it is used to check that data has been double-entered correctly – the sum of the debit and credit balances should be equal. If they are not, it shows that with at least one transaction one or both of the values has been entered wrongly or in the wrong column, or has been omitted altogether.

In a Sage system this cannot happen as the value entered for a transaction is automatically posted to two accounts – once as a debit and once as a credit. However, the trial balance is still useful as it gives a convenient summary of the trading figures. If the credit and debit totals didn't balance it would show that the data had become corrupted.

Profit and Loss account

One of the main uses of the information in your accounts is to assess the profitability of your business – and to find ways to make it more profitable. The Profit and Loss account is a key tool for this. It shows the totals of those accounts that are most directly related to trading, and from these it calculates the current stock levels and the gross and net profit.

♦ **Stock**: purchases plus the difference between the opening and closing stocks.

♦ **Gross Profit**: the difference between your sales income and the cost of goods or raw materials plus the labour and other expenses directly incurred in making and selling the goods.

♦ **Net Profit**: Gross Profit minus office costs and other general overheads.

Bridge Computers
Profit & Loss

	£
Sales	151,837.00
Purchases	62,320.00
Direct Expenses	
Sales Promotion	1,500.00
Gross Profit/(Loss):	88,017.00
Overheads	
Gross Wages	53,950.00
Rent and Rates	3,115.00
Heat, Light and Power	2,000.00
Printing and Stationery	1,500.00
	60,565.00
Net Profit/(Loss):	27,452.00

A simplified Profit & Loss account. This is based on the same figures as the trial balance. In Line 50, the Profit & Loss report will normally show two sets of figures – one for the selected period, and one for the year to date.

End of period adjustments

Even if you are scrupulous in entering all sales and costs as they occur, your end of period accounts may not give a true picture of the business. Some accounts must be adjusted to reflect the reality of the situation. Stock valuation and depreciation must obviously be handled, and when does a debt become a bad debt?

Another problem is that the expenses entered into the accounts may not relate to the period in question. A business may well pay in arrears for some things and in advance for others. In accounting these are called **accruals** and **prepayments**.

Accruals are monies owing for expenses. Rent, rates, power and phone bills are typically paid in arrears. Even if they are paid on receipt, they are unlikely to coincide exactly with the business's year end. The double-entry solution is to set up an *Accruals* account, and to credit end-of-year bills to this, debiting the matching expense. The true total amount of the expense can then be carried into the Profit and Loss account.

A similar *Prepayments* account can be used in the same way, with debits and credits reversed, to handle prepaid bills.

Telephone Account			
Debit	£	Credit	£
Bank	400		
Bank	450		
Bank	450		
Accruals (31/12)	420		
	1720		

Accruals Account		
Debit	£	
		Credit £
		Telephone (31/12) 420

Here the last quarter phone bill was not paid in the financial year, but the cost is taken into the Profit and Loss calculations through the Accruals account.

Accruals and prepayments in Line 50

Line 50 has an Accruals account (Nominal Code 2109) and a Prepayments account (Nominal Code 1103). At the end of the year, any outstanding and pre-paid bills should be posted to these through Journal entries (see page 87).

The balance sheet

The balance sheet provides a summary of the assets and liabilities of a business — and the two totals must balance, or there is something wrong with the calculations!

Bridge Computers
Balance Sheet

	£	£
Fixed Assets		
Plant and Machinery	18,000.00	
Office Equipment	5,400.00	
Furniture and Fixtures	1,240.00	
Motor Vehicles	11,410.00	
		36,050.00
Current Assets		
Stock	11,800.00	
Debtors	7,743.27	
Deposits and Cash	1,200.00	
Bank Account	1,623.30	
		22,366.57
Current Liabilities		
Creditors: Short-term	10,879.75	
VAT Liability	84.82	
		10,964.57
Current Assets less Current Liabilities		11,402.00 #1
Long-term Liabilities	0.00	
Total Assets less Total Liabilities:		**47,452.00**
Capital & Reserves		
Share Capital	20,000.00	
P&L Account	27,452.00	
		47,452.00

A balance sheet based on the same figures as the earlier trial balance and profit and loss account.

#1. The Current Assets less Current Liabilities figure gives an instant check on the liquidity of the business.

Fixed assets are items which have been bought to be retained within the business (for at least a year), and not for resale at a profit. They include equipment, vehicles, property and the like. Any depreciation – or appreciation in value – is entered into the accounts at the end of the period so that a realistic value is present in the balance sheet.

Current assets are those which should be realized (turned into cash) during the year's trading. They are listed in the balance sheet in order of liquidity, with the least liquid at the top.

Current liabilities are the short-term debts owed by the business – principally, the bank overdraft, suppliers' bills not yet paid, and any wages that are due at that point.

Long-term liabilities are loans, mortgages and other debts that will be paid off in instalments over time.

Capital and **Reserves** include share capital and investment by the owner(s). The profit also sits here until it is distributed to the owners or shareholders, or reinvested in the business.

There are two crucial measures that can be drawn from the current assets and liabilities figures.

The **Liquidity Ratio** is a measure of how well a business can find the cash it needs to meet its short-term debts. It is calculated by the simple formula:

$$\text{Liquidity Ratio} = \frac{\text{Current Assets}}{\text{Current Liabilities}}$$

If the ratio is less than 1.0, the business is in trouble. In the Sage Balance Sheet display, the **Current Assets less Liabilities** figure gives a similar guide – this should be a positive value.

In practice, the **Quick Assets Ratio** is a better guide to the ability of a business to survive a crisis. This uses only the most liquid assets and short-term liabilities – those things that can be turned into cash in a hurry:

$$\frac{\text{Cash + Debtors + Cashable Deposits}}{\text{Short-Term Current Liabilities}}$$

Summary

- Businesses of all sizes and types share a common basis and this is reflected in the structure of the accounts.

- The purpose of accounts is to track the flow of money through the business, to help its managers run it more efficiently, and to provide legally required information to the taxman, VAT man and, where appropriate, Companies House.

- Double-entry bookkeeping is based on the concept that every transaction is recorded twice — showing where the money went and where it came from.

- Where sales and purchases are made on credit, transactions with customers are recorded in the Sales Ledger, those with suppliers in the Purchase Ledger.

- The Nominal Ledger is the heart of the bookkeeping system. It should contain separate accounts to record each type of income and expenditure.

- In a manual system the trial balance acts as an important check on the accuracy of entries. In Sage systems, it is a useful source of summary information.

- The Profit and Loss account shows the performance of the business.

- The Balance Sheet provides a summary of the total assets and liabilities of the business, and shows its current value.

02 the Line 50 system

In this chapter you will learn:

- about the Line 50 screen
- how to enter and edit data
- about file maintenance and backups
- about wizards and smartlinks
- how to create and edit reports

2.1 Active Setup

If Line 50 has already been installed on your computer, skip ahead to 2.2. If not, go and find the CD and the rest of the packaging – there's something you'll need in there – and install it now. This should be a simple, straightforward job. The software will install itself from the CD – just respond to the prompts, and let it get on with the job. Unless you choose otherwise, the software will be stored in the *Program Files* folder, in a folder called *Sage*, and a submenu called *Sage Accounts* will be created in the *Programs* area of the Start menu.

The first time that you run Line 50, the ActiveSetup Wizard will appear. You must work through this to activate the software and to write your key company details into it. Before you start, make sure that you have these things at hand:

◆   The serial number and activation key – you should find these in the box, either on a sheet marked 'Important Information' or inside the cover of the User's Guide.

◆   Your company's contact details, financial year start date, and VAT registration number. If the company uses the VAT Cash Accounting scheme, there is an option to set during the setup. If necessary, check with your accountant or your local VAT office before running the Wizard.

If you are setting up Line 50 for the first time, the Wizard will create a basic set of nominal ledger accounts. But different types of business need different structures of accounts – a lawyer won't have retail sales or need to record products in stock – so make sure that you pick the type of company which best matches yours when you reach the My Company stage. The set of accounts probably won't be exactly as you want it, but it will form a solid basis which you can later add to or adapt to meet your needs (see Chapter 3).

1   At the **Welcome** screen click [Next].

2   At **Program Activation**, enter your serial number and activation key.

3   At **My Company**, select a setup for a new company or an upgrade. If this is a new setup, pick the type of business.

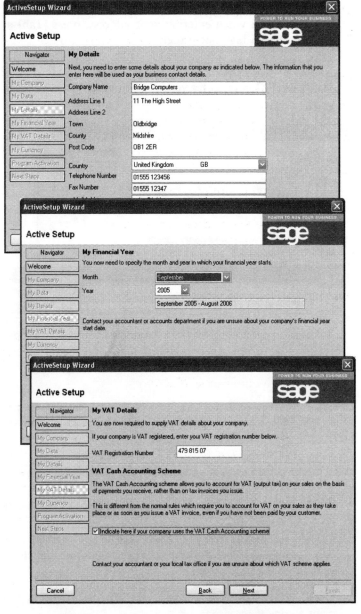

Working through the Active Setup Wizard. If the company is VAT registered,
note the VAT Cash Accounting scheme option at the **My VAT Details** stage.

4 At **My Details**, enter your contact details. Note a peculiarity of this routine: when entering your address, press [**Tab**] at the end of each line, not [**Enter**].

5 At **My Financial Year,** pick the month when your year starts.

6 At **My VAT Details,** enter your VAT number.

7 At **My Currency,** select the currency used for billing.

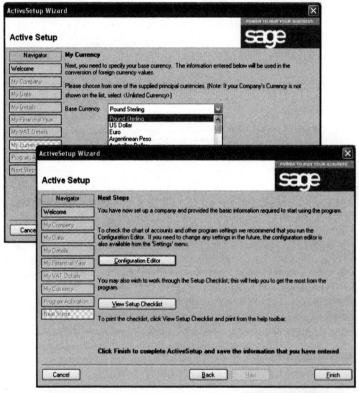

8 At **Next Steps,** if you have time, click `Configuration Editor` to adjust your default settings. These can be left until later, as you can start the Configuration Editor at any time. We'll look at them in the next chapter.

9 Click `View Setup Checklist` to display the checklist. Read it, and print a copy if required.

10 Back at the wizard, click `Finish`.

2.2 The screen display

For anyone who has used Windows – and that must be almost everyone – much of the screen display and the way you interact with it will be immediately obvious. However, the system does have a few little wrinkles all of its own.

Let's start by looking round the main window.

• The **display area** occupies the most space. It is mainly used for listing and selecting records. Data entry and display of the details of accounts of transactions are normally done in dialog boxes or in seperate windows.

• The **tools** above the display area vary to suit the contents.

Tasks list

Links list

Tools

Display area

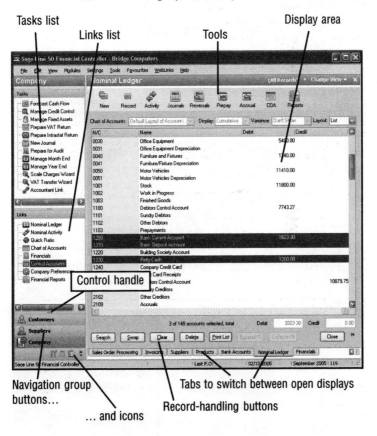

Control handle

Navigation group buttons...

... and icons

Tabs to switch between open displays

Record-handling buttons

- **Buttons** for common record management jobs will be present in the display area if it contains a list.

- If several lists are open at the same time, each will be identified by a tab at the bottom of the display area. Click on a tab to bring its list to the front.

- The **navigation bar** occupies the left of the window.

- The **Customers, Suppliers, Company, Bank** and **Products** buttons are used to navigate between the groups of operations. They can be shown in full, with text labels, or as icons only on the bar beneath.

- The **Tasks list** shows the tasks that are directly related to the current navigation group. Some of these will produce lists in the display area, others will open dialog boxes or new windows for data entry or analysis.

- The **Links list** leads to operations that are in both the current and in other navigation groups. (The distinction between tasks and links eludes me!)

You can adjust the width of the navigation bar and the depth of each of its sections.

To adjust the width:

1 Move the pointer over the dividing line until it changes to a double-headed arrow.

2 Click on the line, hold down the mouse button and drag the guideline in or out.

3 Release the mouse button.

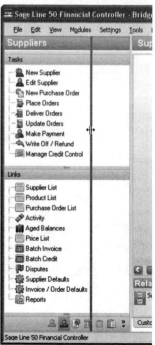

To change the depth of a section:

1 Click on the handle at the top of the section.

2 Drag it up or down as required.

♦ If you shrink the lower section, the buttons will be replaced by icons on the bar beneath.

```
Customers
Suppliers
Sage Line 50 Financial Controller
```

Practise first!

Play with Line 50 before you start to use it in earnest. Start Instant Accounts and use **File > Open > Demo Data** to open the practice files. Explore and experiment with these to get the hang of the system. Later, whenever you are faced with a new operation and are not sure how it works, use the demo files again for practice.

2.3 Viewing records and transactions

The records of any active account will contain a number of transactions over a period of time, but the account can normally be simplified down to a single figure to express its current status. The records of transactions, such as invoices, may similarly have several levels of complexity – there may be a number of items in an invoice, they may not all be paid for at once, some may be returned, etc. Sometimes you want the simple summary, other times you want to get deeper into the record. Opening up deeper levels of details is known as 'drilling down'.

As a general rule, if you have a list of records or transactions on screen and want to look at one in more detail, double-clicking on it will display it in the next level of detail. This does not always work, and sometimes there are alternatives, but both these situations are easily recognized.

♦ In the Customers, Suppliers and similar lists, you will see a Record button in the toolbar. Clicking this will open a window to display the currently selected record. (If several records are selected, it will initially display the topmost. [Next] will bring the next record into view.)

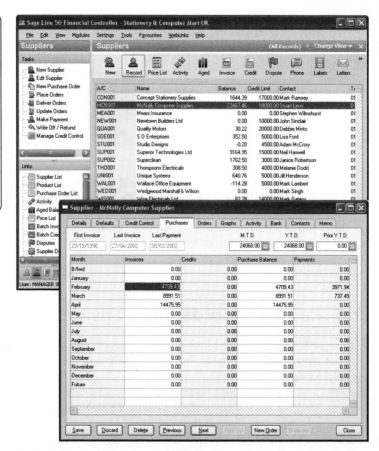

Double-click a record, or select it and click the record button to display it in the next level of detail. Use the [Next] and [Previous] buttons to bring other selected records into the display window.

- In the displays of invoices and similar records of transactions, you may see a ⊞ sign to the left of a transaction. This indicates that there are hidden details. Click on the ⊞ to open it up and display those details. The sign will change to ⊟. Click on this if you want to fold the details away.

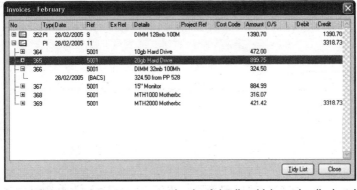

A transaction may have one or more levels of details which can be displayed – look for the ⊞ signs.

2.4 Entering data

For the most part, you use the standard Windows techniques – i.e. type in your text, using backspace to rub out errors, and the arrow keys to move around within text to erase or add new characters. However, there are also a few special techniques that you should learn.

Text items

You very rarely write continuous text when doing the accounts. Almost all text will be short items – names, addresses and other details of new customers, entries on invoices, and the like. Each of these items will normally go into a separate field (text box) on screen.

* If you have something that you want to spread over several lines, such as the details in a service invoice, press [Enter] at the end of each line.

* When you want to go to the next field, press [Tab].

* If you need to go back to a field to correct an entry, hold [Shift] and press [Tab].

Number entry

Click to bring tab to the front

Drop-down list

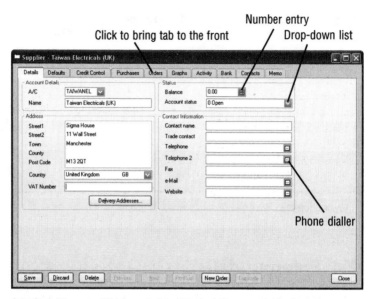

A typical data entry/display window. Most of these are tabbed windows –
click on the label to bring its tab to the front.

Easy data entry

Line 50 provides easy ways to enter numbers, dates and any
information that is already in your files.

Numbers

Backspace   Clear entry

When you go to a number field, you will
usually see ▦ by the side. Click on this
and a small calculator will appear. Click on the
digits to enter a number or use it as a calculator
to work out discounts or other values. Click ▤
to show the result and exit.

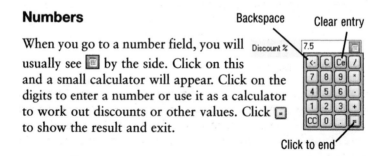

Phone dialler

Click to end

With simple numbers, e.g. due days, there
may be a pair of little arrows on the right of
the field. Click on these to increase or decrease the value.

Dates

The Program Date (normally the current date, but see page 70) is entered automatically into date fields. If you want to change it, click 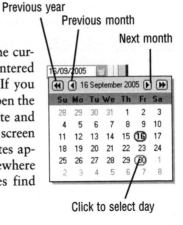 to open the 'calendar' display. Select the date and press [Esc] or click elsewhere on screen to close the calendar. These dates appear in Day/Month order; elsewhere in the system you'll sometimes find them in Month/Day order.

Previous year
Previous month
Next month

Click to select day

Drop-down lists

When you are creating an invoice and need the details of a customer, then – as long as it is already in the system – the information can be pulled out by selecting from the list that drops down from the at the side of the field. Accounts, names of suppliers, product details and similar data can likewise be selected from drop-down lists.

2.5 Selections

Before you can edit, delete or in any other way process a record or account, it must be selected. This is done by clicking anywhere on its line in its window.

Multiple selection

In the Customers, Suppliers, Nominal, Products and Invoicing windows, any number of records can be selected at any one time – and once selected, a record stays selected until you deselect it. This is a valuable feature as it allows you to process records in batches.

For example, one of your first jobs when setting up Line 50 will be to work through the Nominal accounts entering opening balances. If you first go through the list and select all the relevant ones, you can then work steadily through the opening balances routine without having to keep coming back to select the next record.

To select multiple records:

1   Click on them! (That's it, no need to hold down [Ctrl] as in most Windows applications.)

2   If you want all but a few of the records, select the ones you don't want, then click [Swap] to invert the selection.

3   If you select one by mistake, click on it again to deselect.

4   If you have selected several then decide that you do not want them, you can deselect them all by clicking [Clear].

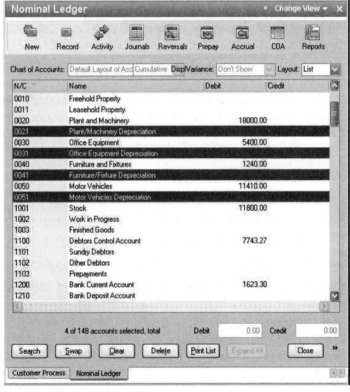

Selecting a batch of records for processing.

Single selection

Only one record can be selected at a time in the Bank and Financial modules. Clicking on a record automatically deselects any other selection. Similarly, only one item can be selected in the panels that display the details of records. In most of these cases, 'selecting' a record or item does no more than highlight it for easier identification, as they cannot be edited or processed.

2.6 Wizards

Wizards are routines designed to help you perform operations that might otherwise be tricky. You will meet them when you first set up Line 50 for your system, whenever you create a new customer, supplier or other account, when you are doing transfers and adjustments within your Nominal Ledger, and in similar situations. At the very least, they help to ensure that you supply the right kind of information and that it goes into the right place.

The examples here are from the Customer Record Wizard, but all wizards work in much the same way. With the information gathering wizards, such as this one, it is best if you have all the necessary information on hand at the start. However, if you don't have it, or don't have time to complete working through the wizard, it won't matter too much, as the record can be edited and new data added at any time.

1 Start the wizard. In this case, if the Customer List is open click [New], otherwise click [Customers] to go to the Customers navigation group, then select **New Customer** in the **Tasks**.

2 Read the prompts and enter information or select optional settings where indicated.

3 Click [Next] to go on to the next panel.

4 If you want to correct an error, click [Back] to return to the panel.

5 If you decide to abandon the operation, click [Cancel].

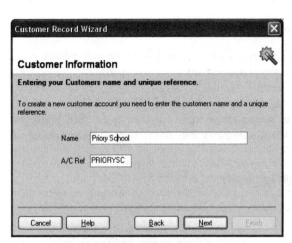

An early stage of the Customer Record Wizard.

Underlined items have explanations attached

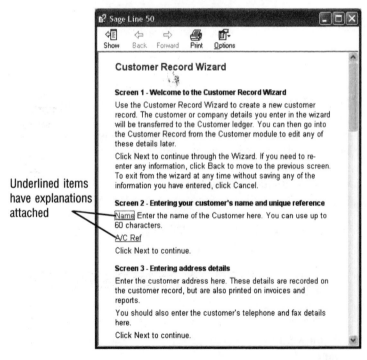

The Help page that is displayed by the Help button in the Customer Record Wizard. If any text is blue and underlined, you can click on it to get an explanation of what it is or what is required of you at that point.

6 If you are not sure what to do at any stage, click [Help].

7 At the last panel, click [Finish] to save your information.

The window warning

This is a minor point, but worth noting as it can throw you the first time you meet it. When you select some routines, you will see a Confirm dialog box, warning you that all open windows must be closed and any unsaved data may be lost. This only refers to windows **within** the Sage system – if you are also running a browser or word processor or other application at the same time, it will not be affected.

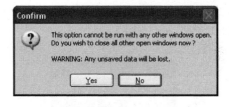

2.7 Smart links

Smart links offer a direct connection to related records. For example, when compiling a sales order, you may need to check or change some details in the customer's record. You could reach that record by going back into the main display, then opening it from the customer list, but there's a quicker way. Next to the customer's account reference, there is a fat yellow arrow ⬯. This is a smart link. Click on it and the customer's record window will open immediately.

Smart link —————

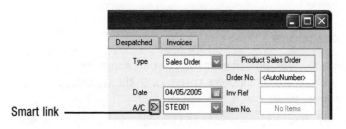

2.8 File maintenance

All data needs a certain amount of maintenance to be kept in good order. Line 50 has a set of commands to help maintain your data. One of these should be used as a matter of routine, four will probably be needed from time to time, and there's one that you will hope that you never have to use in earnest!

• Open the **File** menu and select **Maintenance...** to display the **File Maintenance** dialog box. All the operations start from here.

Check data

The Check data routine will scan your files, and the links between them, to make sure that your data is in good order. If all is well – and it almost certainly will be – you will get this message:

If things have gone awry, the File Maintenance Problems Report window will be displayed. The Summary will give you an overview. To get the details of any errors, warnings or comments, switch to the appropriate tab. There is a Fix facility that should be able to correct the errors, but if this doesn't work it almost certainly means that your files are corrupted and should be restored from the backups (see page 38).

Warnings and comments, if any, will normally relate to minor inconsistencies which you should be able to correct from within the system.

Corrections

If an error is made when entering a transaction, or a transaction is cancelled after it has been entered into the system, you may be able to delete or edit it through the Corrections routine.

• Bank transfers (page 161) and Journal entries (page 87), which have matching double-entries, cannot be deleted and you can only edit non-critical information, such as Department codes and descriptive text.

- If you cannot correct the errors here, you can issue credit notes to nullify invoices or make Journal entries to reverse mispostings.

1 Click [Corrections].

2 Select the transaction and click [Edit].

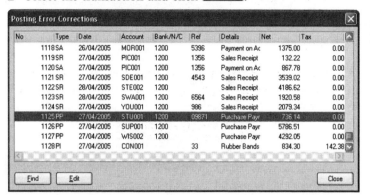

No	Type	Date	Account	Bank/N/C	Ref	Details	Net	Tax	
1118	SA	26/04/2005	MOR001	1200	5396	Payment on Ac	1375.00	0.00	
1119	SR	27/04/2005	PIC001	1200	1356	Sales Receipt	132.22	0.00	
1120	SA	27/04/2005	PIC001	1200	1356	Payment on Ac	867.78	0.00	
1121	SR	27/04/2005	SDE001	1200	4543	Sales Receipt	3539.02	0.00	
1122	SR	28/04/2005	STE002	1200		Sales Receipt	4186.62	0.00	
1123	SR	28/04/2005	SWA001	1200	6564	Sales Receipt	1920.58	0.00	
1124	SR	27/04/2005	YOU001	1200	986	Sales Receipt	2079.34	0.00	
1125	PP	27/04/2005	STU001	1200	09871	Purchase Payr	736.14	0.00	
1126	PP	27/04/2005	SUP001	1200		Purchase Payr	5786.51	0.00	
1127	PP	27/04/2005	WIS002	1200		Purchase Payr	4292.05	0.00	
1128	PI	27/04/2005	CON001		33	Rubber Bands	834.30	142.38	

[Find] [Edit]   [Close]

3 If the transaction has not been reconciled on the VAT return, if can be deleted – click [Delete] if you want to do this.

- **Editing transactions**

4 Edit information in the **Details** area as needed.

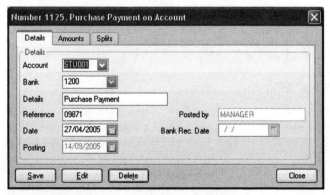

Number 1125, Purchase Payment on Account

| Details | Amounts | Splits |

Details

Account   STU001

Bank   1200

Details   Purchase Payment

Reference 09871   Posted by   MANAGER

Date   27/04/2005   Bank Rec. Date   / /

Posting   14/09/2005

[Save] [Edit] [Delete]   [Close]

5 To edit the amounts, switch to the **Splits** tab, select the line and click [Edit].

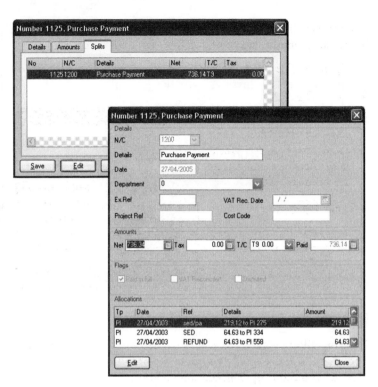

6 Edit the **Details** and **Amounts** as needed.

7 Click [Close] to leave the **Split Record** panel.

8 Click [Save] to write the changes to the files. You will be prompted to confirm that you really want to do this.

9 Click [Close].

Compression

When transactions, records and other data items are deleted – either through corrections or, more commonly, as part of clearing the audit trail (see page 168) – the data initially remains in the files, but is flagged so that it is ignored by the system. The compression routine works through the files, removing all those records marked as 'deleted'. It is something that should be done from time to time to save disk space and to improve the efficiency of your data-handling.

Always run the Check Data routine first. If there are problems in the files, they should be found and fixed before compression.

1 Open the **File** menu and click **Maintenance**.

2 Click [Compress Data].

3 If you only want to compress certain files, clear the **Compress All Data Files** checkbox and select the required files.

4 Click [Compress].

5 You will be told when compression is complete. Click [Close] to exit the routine.

ReIndex

Indexing allows a data file to be searched more efficiently – and note that the index is only visible to the progam, and not to you. Over time, additions, deletions and alterations to a file make the index less cleanly structured and less efficient to use. There may come a point where reindexing is worth considering. However, this is not to be undertaken lightly, as the process can damage the files! If you know that the files have undergone a lot of changes, and it seems to be taking ever longer to pull up records from the files, contact customer support and discuss reindexing with them before doing anything.

Rebuild

Also not to be used lightly – in fact, not to be used at all in normal circumstances! This routine erases all your data files so that you can start again from scratch. The only time that you would probably want to use this would be after you have been working with the dummy data to get the hang of the system. Rebuild clears away the rubbish ready to start work in earnest.

Logging

The logging button displays the View Event Log window which lists the maintenance jobs that have been done on the files.

2.9 Backups

Once you start to use Line 50 in earnest, you must get into the habit of backing up your files regularly. The Sage system is very reliable but computers get stolen or damaged, and hard disks can fail. Would your business survive if it lost all its accounts data? More specifically, how much data can you afford to lose and still survive?

A backup file will store that precious accounts data – it will also hold your configuration settings and company details. Backups should be made:

• Daily, or at most weekly, depending upon the number of trans-actions going through the accounts.

• On removable media, stored away from the computer, in a fireproof safe, and preferably in another building.

• With each backup on a separate disk or tape, so that if one is destroyed or corrupted, there is a recent previous version to work from. If you do daily backups, you might have a set of 5 (or 6) that you recycle weekly.

If you have not backed up recently, you will be prompted when you close down Line 50. But don't wait for the prompt – get into the habit.

1 Open the **File** menu and select **Backup...**

2 Select the drive and directory, and edit the name as required.

3 Tick or clear the checkboxes to select the file types to backup.

4 Click [OK].

5 Wait while the files are saved – this could take some time.

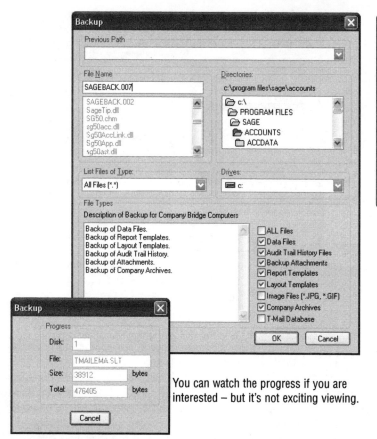

You can watch the progress if you are interested – but it's not exciting viewing.

Restoring files

If the worst happens and you have a hard disk crash or lose the data in any other way, you can recreate the files – if necessary on a new computer – using the Restore routine.

You will lose all the transactions that have been recorded since the backup, but if you have been maintaining the files properly and backing up regularly, they should not take long to re-enter.

1 Open the **File** menu and select **Restore...**

2 You will almost certainly be asked to confirm that you want to do this – an unnecessary restore will make a lot of extra work for nothing.

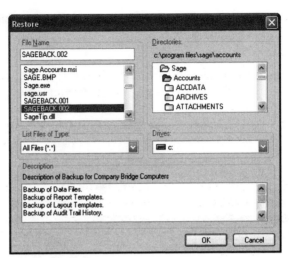

3 The last backup should be already selected. If this is not the one you want, use the Drive, Directory and File Name selectors to locate the file.

4 Click [OK].

5 Wait while the files are copied back into place. This could take a while so you may as well take a break.

Which backup?

You normally restore from the most recent backup, though you may have to use an earlier one, if the files had been corrupted – without anyone noticing – at the time of the last backup (which is why you should check the data first).

2.10 Task Manager

Task Manager is a reminder system, and one with limited functions. Only the To Do and Bills sections are interactive – in these you can create, edit and delete reminders and other items. The rest only display information – you can see the appropriate records, but you cannot do anything with them, except change the telephone number of a contact. The Task Manager listing is a convenient way of seeing which invoices and payments are due or overdue, but to record the payment of an overdue invoice, you need go to the appropriate routine in the Customers, Suppliers or Bank modules.

The Tasks buttons down the left side are used to move between the sections: To Do, Bills, Accounts Due, Accounts Status, Recurring, Stock, Invoices, and Sales and Purchase Orders. The adjacent folder list displays the subsections of the selected task, and the items in the current folder are listed in the main pane.

1 Open the **File** menu and select **Task Manager**.

2 Click the **Task** button. If you can't see the one you want, use the scroll arrows at the top or bottom to bring it into view.

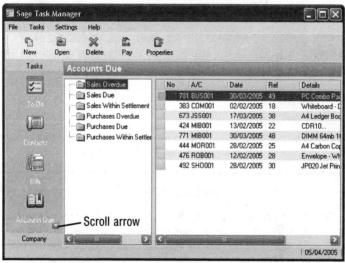

3 Select a subsection from the folder display.

4 Double-click on an item to view its details in a new window.

5 Use the [First], [Previous], [Next] and [Last] buttons to look at other items in the folder, if required.

6 Click [OK] to close the window.

To create a new To Do task:

1 Go to the **To Do** section.

2 Click the **New** button.

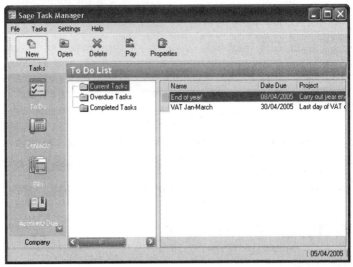

3 For the **Type**, click the drop-down arrow and select a type from the list.

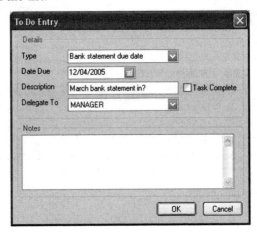

4   Type the **Date Due,** or use the calendar tool to set the date.

5   Enter a **Description.** This is essential – even though the Type may say pretty well all you wanted to say about the reminder.

6   If there are several users on the system, you can select the one to **Delegate** the task to.

7   If it will be useful, add some **Notes.**

8   Click [OK].

If necessary you can reopen the item later – double-click it, or select it and click the **Open** button – and edit the details. When the job is done, reopen the item and tick the **Task complete** box. This will remove it from the list.

Company details

The Company label, at the bottom of the Tasks list simply displays the basic company information. You cannot edit the details from here.

2.11 Report Designer

Line 50 has a wide selection of ready-made letters, statements and other document formats which should be adequate for most accounting purposes. However, they are standardized, and may not be quite what you need. If required you can edit them – you may want to add the Balance to your reminder letters – or create your own documents from scratch. The same Report Designer window opens, whether you are working on a label, letter, statement or report.

You can get into the Report Designer in two ways.

All the module windows have toolbar buttons for letters, reports or whatever layouts are available in that module. The dialog boxes that open from these are mainly used to select layouts for printing, but they can also be edited from here.

Use the Reports Wizard to edit a template or to create a new one of your own.

A layout document is made up of elements:

+ **Text** 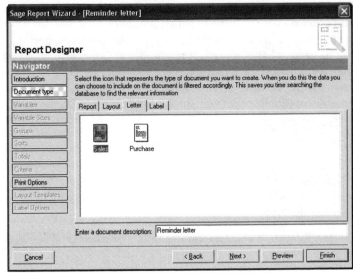, written in separate boxes – the box will expand as you type. The text can be formatted as in Word.

+ **Variables** which draw data from your files. They are grouped by origin, so there are, for example, one set relating to customer accounts, another to your company's details.

+ **Lines** and **boxes** , for marking off areas.

+ **Expressions** (calculations on fields) started from .

+ **Images**, such as your company logo, inserted from .

Starting from the Wizard

This is the hardest, but if you can build a report – even a simple one – from scratch, then you will have no problems about editing and reformatting a ready-made one.

1 Open the **File** menu, point to **New** and select **Report...**

2 At the Report Wizard, click on the **Document Type** button, in the set on the left, then go to either the **Report, Layout, Letter** or **Label** tab and select a basic template.

3 Type a **Description** and click [Next].

4 At the next stage, set the **Paper size** and click [Finish].

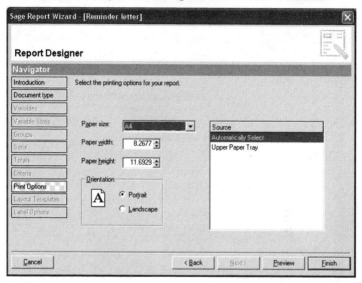

5 The **Report Designer** window will open. At first, there will only be a slim area at the top. Drag the footer line down to expand the **Details** area – this is where we will write a letter.

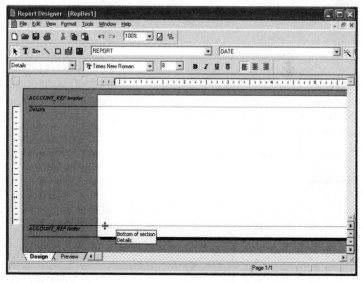

Insert text box   Insert variable   Zoom   Formatting tools

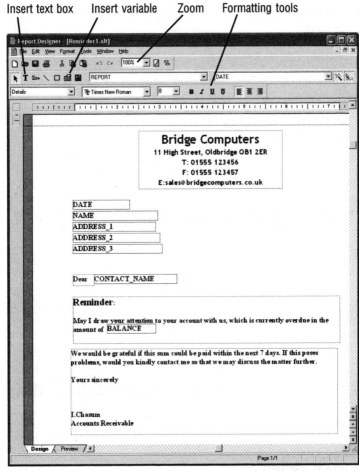

The Report Designer window, with a 'report' – in this case, a letter – almost complete. The variables are labelled in CAPITALS, for easy identification. They can be formatted as ordinary text, and can be spliced into – or on top of – a text box, though perfect alignment is tricky!

Adding text

1   Click **T** then drag a rectangle approximately where you want the text to appear. It can be moved or resized later.

2   Type your text. If there is too much to fit, drag on the bottom or right edge of the box to expand it.

3 Click anywhere out of the box to end the text-entry mode.

4 To format the text, you must first select it:

To select all text in the box, click once on the box.

To select a block of text, click once in the box to make it active, then click and drag over the text.

5 Use the buttons in the Formatting toolbar to set the font, size, emphasis or alignment.

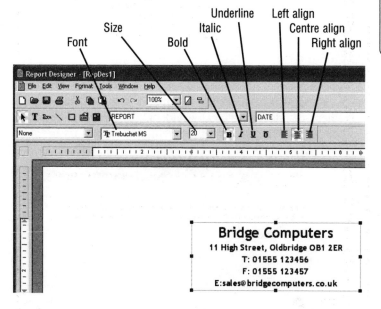

Adding variables

1 Click .

2 Select the table to draw the data from, e.g. the COMPANY table for data from your own business, or SALES LEDGER for customer data.

3 Select the variable.

4 Click and drag onto the form to draw an outline rectangle where you want the data to go.

Data table

Variable

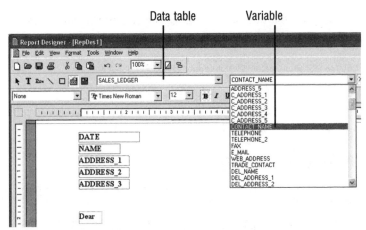

5 The **Active Complete** dialog box will open. This can add a title and/or a total for the variable, if required. In a report, where the data is typically laid out in rows and columns, titles and totals are often wanted; on a letter, a variable is more likely to be placed as a single item by itself.

No titles in a letter

Title above a column of data...

...or to the left of a single one.

You can set the size exactly, or just drag the box to size

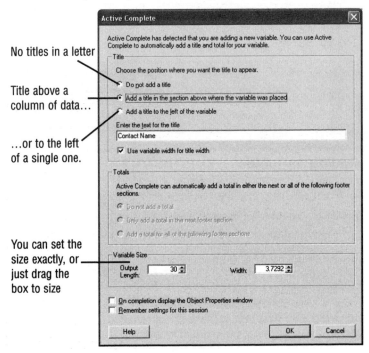

6 Drag on the handles to change the size of the variable's display box, or click anywhere on the box and drag to move it.

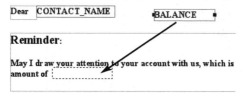

Adding lines and boxes

Lines and boxes are useful for separating areas in a long report, or for making things stand out in a report or letter.

1 Click [\] for a line or [□] for a box.

2 Click where you want one end of the line/corner of the box.

3 Drag across to the other end/corner.

4 The object can be resized by dragging on a handle, or moved by dragging anywhere else on the line/in the box.

Page Setup

You may want to change the margins, as the defaults are small.

1 Open the **File** menu and select **Page Setup**.

2 On the Margins tab, set new margins either by typing or with the little arrows on the right. Line 50 normally uses inches – you can change to centimetres in the **Tools > Options** dialog box.

3 Click [OK].

Use the **adjustments** and **scaling** to print reports accurately on printed stationery – adjustment values change the top left point at which printing starts; scaling percentages set the width and height of the print area.

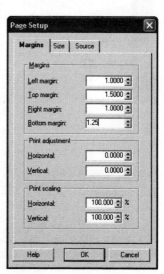

Print preview

Previewing before you print is always a good idea – especially when you have started from scratch. Things to check:

Are variable boxes wide enough to fit their data?

Do variables line up properly with text in text boxes?

Is the spacing between boxes balanced?

Use **File > Print Preview** to start, and close the window when you have done.

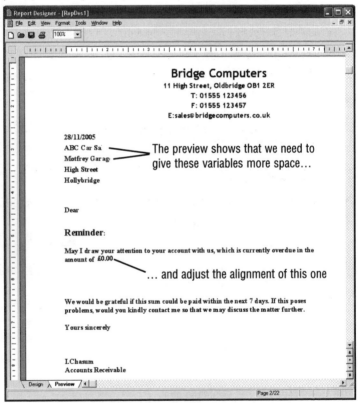

Save it!

Don't forget to save your report design when you have finished – you'll need it later.

Summary

- There are some neat tools to simplify data entry. Numbers can be entered (after calculating, if needed) through a mini-calculator; dates through a calendar; and account codes through drop-down lists.

- Records are selected by clicking on them. In most module windows, any number of records can be selected for processing in a batch.

- There are wizards to guide you through some of the trickier jobs.

- Smart links offer a direct connection to related records.

- The data maintenance routines should keep your data files in good order...

- ...but you must take regular backups, to safeguard against loss of data.

- You may find the Task Manager useful for reminding you of jobs that need doing.

- You can create new reports, or edit existing layouts using Report Designer.

03

setting up the accounts

In this chapter you will learn:

- how to configure Line 50 to suit your business
- about the preferences and other default settings
- how to change the program date or password

3.1 Details and defaults

You will have set up some of the details and defaults for your company during installation. Default settings for customers and suppliers, the organization of the business into departments and of products into categories, may also have been set up then. Any information that was not entered then, or has changed since, can be put in through the Configuration Editor or the Company Preferences options.

The Configuration Editor

The Configuration Editor dialog box has a dozen tabs. Only the General tab needs immediate attention, and there are another two that we will have a look at now. We'll work through the rest as we cover the parts of the system to which they apply.

Configuration templates

Line 50 comes with templates with the basic configurations for 10 different types of business. Use one to speed up your setup – it will apply the industry-standard chart of accounts, terms of business, tax codes and the like to your accounts system.

1 Open the **Settings** menu and select **Configuration...**

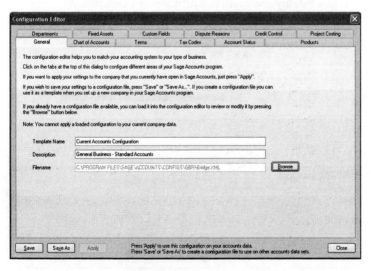

2   On the **General** tab, click 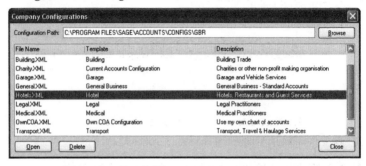 Browse to open the **Company Con-figurations** dialog box.

3   Scroll through the list and select the most suitable template for your business.

4   Click ⌐ Open ⌐ to apply the template.

Departments

If your company is organized into departments, or has several branches, these can be written into the Line 50 system and used when creating invoices and analysing activity. Even if there are no actual departments, it can be useful to set up 'virtual' departments for each area of the firm's work, as this will enable you to see more easily the relative profitability of each.

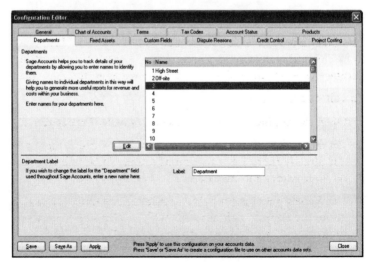

To set up departments:

1 Switch to the **Departments** tab.

2 Select an unused field and click  Edit .

Edit Department ✕

No   3

Name   Mail order

OK   Cancel

3 Type a name for the department and click OK .

4 Repeat to set up as many departments as you need.

Fixed Assets

You may find it useful to organize fixed assets into categories, because, as with departments, this can improve the quality of the analysis. Spend a little time thinking about this before doing anything, and don't forget that there will be a number of fixed assets accounts in any case. Categories are worth setting up if there are many fixed assets accounts, which could be grouped for more efficient handling in reports.

Creating asset categories is the same as creating departments.

Company Preferences

The **Company Preferences** dialog box has five panels. Two need to be checked and perhaps changed now – the **Address** and the **Parameters** – especially if several people work on the accounts.

To edit and set preferences:

1 Open the **Settings** menu and select **Company Preferences...**

2 On the **Address** panel, enter your contact details, if these are not already there from the initial setup. These will be used on your letters and invoices.

3 The **Labels** panel is probably best left alone until you really know the system. This controls which fields are included in the customer, supplier and product records.

4 On the **Parameters** panel, set your VAT defaults and other options as required. If more than one person will be keeping the accounts, and you want to set limits to which parts of the accounts they can access and change, turn on Access Rights.

If you want to create users and set their levels of access, you must first enable Access Rights in the Company Preferences dialog box.

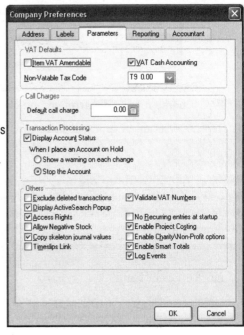

5 The **Reporting** tab sets basic defaults for printed reports and letters and the format for e-mails.

6 The **Accountant** tab holds the contact details of the firm's accountant.

7 When you have worked through the tabs, click OK.

3.2 Multiple users and access rights

Where several people work on the accounts, and if they have different responsibilities or different levels of skill, you may need to restrict their access to certain areas and/or to certain tasks within areas. Sage gives you a way to set precise limits to access. The process is – frankly – fiddly, but should only need to be done once for each person – or once for each job specification where several people have the same responsibilities and the same access limits.

1 Turn on **Access Rights** in the **Company Preferences**.

2 Open the **Settings** menu and select **Access Rights...**

3 Click [New] to create a new user.

4 Enter a **Logon Name** and **Password**.

5 At this point there appears to be a simple two-way choice on access rights – **Full Access** or **No Access**. This is simply a starting point and you can add or remove specific access rights at the next stage. If the user is to have access to most areas, select **Full Access**; if not, select **No Access**.

6 Click [Save] to save the user's data.

7 The **Logon Name** and **Password** fields will clear and you can create another user. It is probably better to complete the first one before you start another. Click [Close].

8 Back at the **User Access Rights** dialog box, select the newly-created user and click [De_tails].

9 You can set access rights to whole modules, or to dialogs – the windows in which tasks are carried out.

To set access at module level:

10 Click [Modules].

To select a lot of options, it is quicker to select the ones you don't want and click Swap to reverse the selection.

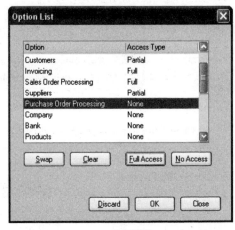

11 Select the module(s) to set, then click [Full Access] or [No Access].

12 Click [OK] to save the settings – you will be prompted for confirmation.

To set access at dialog level:

13 Select the module containing the relevant dialogs.

14 Click [Dialogs].

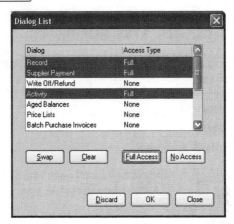

15 Select the operations(s) to set, then click [Full Access] or [No Access].

16 Save and exit as before.

Creating users by copying

On the **User Access Rights** dialog box you will see [Copy]. You can use this to create a new user with the same access rights as an existing one. Now you see why I suggested finishing on the first user before starting the second! Even if the rights are a little different from any other user, starting from a similar level will often be quicker than starting from scratch.

1 On the **User Access Rights** dialog box, select the user with the closest set of access rights.

2 Click [Copy].

3 Enter the **Logon Name** and **Password** to create the user and click [OK].

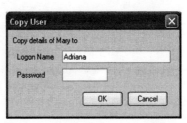

4 Back at the **User Access Rights** dialog box, select the copied user and click [Details].

5 Make any necessary changes at module or dialog level.

3.3 Customers and suppliers

The Customers and Suppliers defaults follow the same pattern – and some of the settings apply to both. They are controlled through the Configuration Editor, and through the Customer and Supplier Defaults dialog boxes.

Configuration Editor

1 Use **Settings > Configuration...** to open the **Configuration Editor,** then work through the tabs as detailed below.

2 Click [Apply] when you are finished to fix the settings.

Terms

What is your normal credit limit for a new customer? When is payment due? Do you offer a discount for early settlement? And what do your suppliers normally set as the limits, due dates and discounts?

Remember that these are only the default settings. When you are creating a new customer or supplier account, you can change the settings as needed.

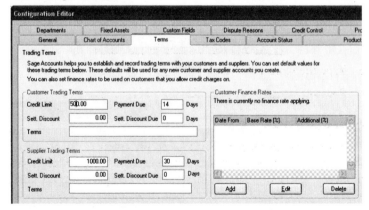

Dispute reasons

If you are in dispute with a customer or supplier, you may find it useful to be able to apply a predefined 'dispute reason' to the account, instead of writing a note. Initially only 'No reason' is defined – you may want to set up a bank of reasons. Whether or not this is worth the time depends upon how often you are likely to be in dispute, so you might want to leave this until later.

To set up dispute reasons:

1 Switch to the **Dispute Reasons** panel.

2 Select an unused line and click [Edit].

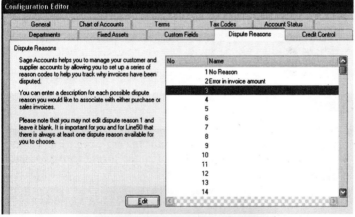

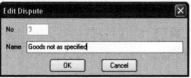

3 Type the reason and click [OK].

4 Repeat to create your standard set of reasons.

Account status

This is similar to Dispute Reasons in providing a set of labels that can be attached to an account, but will almost certainly be of more use to more people. As well as showing the status of the account, these can also be set to put an account on hold.

There are 10 ready-made status descriptions – mostly relating to problem accounts, and these are all set so that the account is put on hold when the status is applied.

To change or create an account status:

1 Switch to the **Account Status** panel.

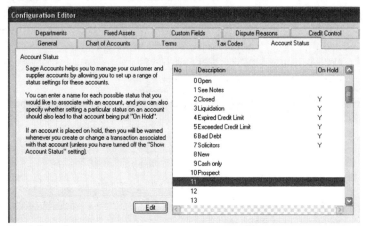

2 Select the status to change, or an unused line to create a new status.

3 Click [Edit].

4 Type a **Description**.

5 If you want these accounts to be marked "On Hold", tick the checkbox.

6 Click [OK].

Customer defaults

1 Use **Settings > Customer Defaults...** to open the **Customer Defaults** dialog box, then work through the tabs.

2 Click [OK] when you have done to fix the settings.

Records

These defaults are applied to new transactions on customers' accounts. They should be set to the most commonly used VAT code, nominal code (N/C), department (if any) and discount rate. Most of these can be set by selecting from a drop-down list.

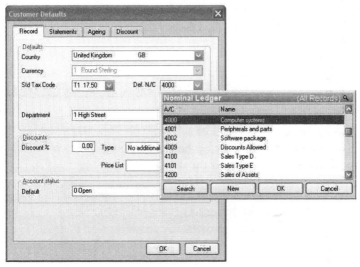

Statements

The Statements panel simply holds the descriptions to be applied to invoices, credit notes and other printouts.

Ageing

Chasing debts efficiently is a key part of good cashflow management. Aged Analysis groups overdue debts, with the default settings in multiples of 30 days. You can switch to calendar month grouping, or set your own limits. At which point do you start counting? How old is a debt before you send a reminder, and how much older before you send for the lawyers?

The Ageing settings are used to select records in the credit control routines. See page 138.

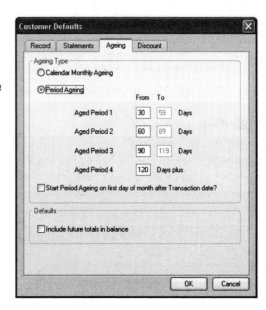

Discounts

If you have standard levels of sales at which you normally apply discounts, they can be set up here. Use the drop-down calculator, or type the values and the discount percentages.

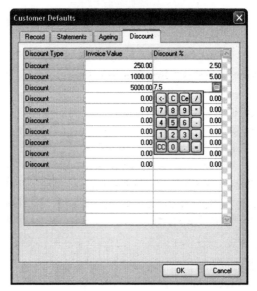

> ### Supplier Defaults
>
> The Supplier Defaults dialog box only has the Record and Ageing panels, which are used as for Customer Defaults.

3.4 Bank accounts

Line 50 comes with a basic set of bank accounts: current and deposit bank accounts, building society account, petty cash and company credit card. More can be set up if need be, and if you are likely to create more than a few, you might want to set the defaults. To do this:

1   Open the **Settings** menu and select **Bank Defaults...**

2   Tick the checkboxes to turn the options on or off.

+   **Group items in Bank Rec.** will display in one line any items where the reference code and date are the same.

+   **List Payment/Receipt by split** shows the individual transactions in an invoice – this is turned on automatically if the company uses VAT cash accounting.

+   **No Warning on Visa receipts** turns off the alert that appears if a receipt is entered against a company credit card account.

+   **Group Bank Transactions** will group all of each day's bank transactions into a single header line.

+   **Always Create Remittance** creates a remittance advice note when you record a supplier payment.

3   Click [OK].

3.5 Products

The Product module provides stock control facilities, but the product information is also used when generating invoices and credit notes – selecting a product's code will pull in its description, price, tax rate and default order quantity. It can take time to enter the details of all your business's products, but it will save more time in the long run. You can speed up data entry by setting appropriate defaults for the products.

Products can be organized into categories. If you have a website where you display or sell your products, these can help your customers to locate items. They can also be useful for analysing your business activities.

If you intend to use categories, they are best created before setting the defaults and before entering the details of products.

1 Open the **Settings** menu, select **Configuration...** and switch to the **Products panel.**

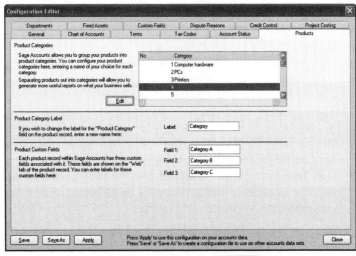

2 Select an unused category and click [Edit].

3 Enter a name and click [OK].

4 Repeat steps 2 and 3 for all your new categories, then click [Apply] to store the definitions in your configuration data, or [Save] to save the new configuration to file.

Product categories

If necessary, a new product category can be set up when you are creating a product record.

To set the product defaults:

1 Open the **Settings** menu and select **Product Defaults...**

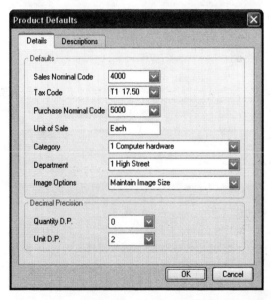

2 Select the most common settings for **Nominal Code, Tax Code, Unit of Sale, Category** and **Department.**

3 Set the number of decimal places to show for **Quantities** and **Prices** on invoices.

4 Click [OK].

3.6 Invoice and order defaults

There are six tabs of settings in the Invoice and Order Defaults dialog box. All need to be checked and changed to suit your business. In particular, you should set the default invoice to the type you use most – product or service, and if you have cash sales, you should select which printouts are to be produced with each sale.

1 From the **Settings** menu select **Invoice & Order Defaults...**

2 On the **General** tab, set the default invoice and sales order format and their related options.

3 On the **Footer Defaults**, set the default net costs and nominal codes for carriage on sales and purchases.

4 On the **Options** tab, set the start points for numbering on the printouts if you want to pick up from existing sequences.

5   On the **Discounts** tab, set the defaults for how and to whom discounts are to apply.

6   If your trade within the EU requires it, switch to the **Instrastat** tab and turn on the reporting options.

7   If you have cash sales, go to the **Cash Sales** tab and set the printing options.

8   Click [OK].

3.7 Financial Year

If necessary, you can change the start month for your financial year. This, of course, has a major impact on the system, so some preparatory work is needed to protect and preserve valuable data. The change will wipe out the prior year values in the Nominal accounts, so if these are required, they should be at least printed out beforehand. And your data must be backed up!

1 Open the **Settings** menu and select **Financial Year...**

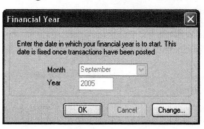

2 The month cannot be changed by simply typing in the new one – click [Change...].

3 You will be prompted to check and backup your data. If you have not done so already, do this now.

4 You will be warned that historical data will be lost. If you want to continue, click [Yes].

5 Select the new start month from the drop-down list and click [OK], then click [OK] again when you get back to the **Financial Year** dialog box.

3.8 Program Date

Whenever a date is required, the current date will be set as the default, but it can be easily changed. If you intend to process a lot of transactions with the same date – and not today's – set the Program Date before you start.

1 Open the **Settings** menu and select **Change Program Date...**

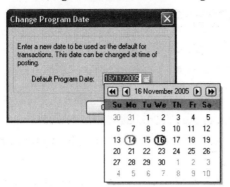

2 Set the date, by typing or by using the calendar display.

3 Set the date and click [OK].

3.9 Change Password

If you need to protect your accounts, you can set a password to be given at the start of every session. The password should be something you won't forget, but one that others will not guess easily. It should be changed regularly for optimum security.

1 Open the **Settings** menu and select **Change Password**.

2 Type the password *twice* – as only asterisks are shown, this avoids mistyping errors.

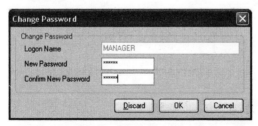

3 In future, the password must be given at the start of each session, and must also be given if you want to change it.

4 If things change and a password is no longer needed, run the Change routine again, and leave the Password fields blank.

Summary

- ♦ To tailor Line 50 to suit your business, you should start by working through the tabs of the Configuration Editor.

- ♦ The details of your business are recorded in the Company Preferences section. As with almost all of the Settings data, they can be changed at any time if necessary.

- ♦ If you set up defaults to suit the majority of your customers and suppliers, it will simplify life when you create new accounts.

- ♦ If you deal in products, you should set up suitable product defaults.

- ♦ Other options on the Settings menu let you change the program date, invoice and order defaults and the password.

04

the company module

In this chapter you will learn:

- about Company tasks and tools
- about the chart of accounts
- how to create Nominal accounts
- about journal entries
- how to view activity
- how to edit report layouts

4.1 Company tasks and tools

The Company module covers all of the Nominal ledger work, except for those tasks that relate to any of the bank accounts. It is here that you define the structure of the accounts, set opening balances, make journal entries and reversals, compile the VAT return and manage your assets. The financial analysis tools and reports, and the end of period routines can also be reached from this module.

Some operations are started from the Tasks or the Links in the left hand panes, others from the toolbar buttons – and some from both.

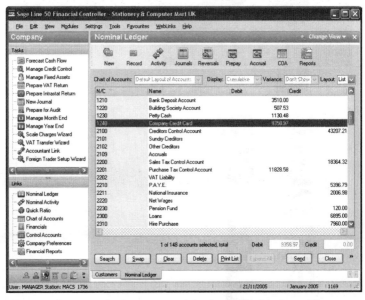

When you first open the Company module, the Nominal Ledger will appear, listing the Nominal accounts and their current balances. Most commonly used operations can be started from the toolbar buttons, and notice the buttons below the display of accounts: Print List will give you a hard copy of the accounts' N/C (Nominal Code), names and balances, and Send will export the same data to Excel.

4.2 Nominal records

Though the Nominal ledger is the heart of the accounting system, once it is set up there are relatively few situations in which you will work on it directly. Most Nominal ledger entries arise from transactions with customers and suppliers, which are normally handled through the Bank (Chapter 7), Customers or Suppliers (Chapter 8) modules.

The Nominal module is mainly used for viewing Nominal records, for performing (fairly rare) journal entries, and for setting up budgets.

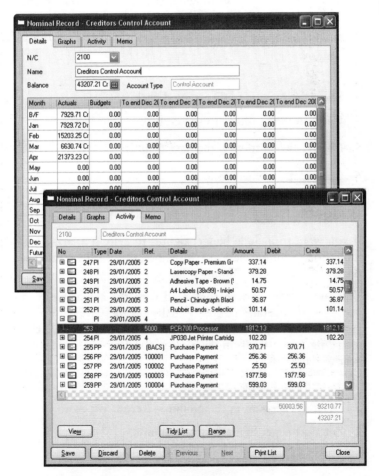

The record panels have four tabs:

* **Details** shows the current balance, and the balance, budget and prior year figures for each month (if present).

* **Graphs** shows the same monthly figures in visual form.

* **Activity** shows the transactions currently in the audit trail for that account.

* **Memo** is a free space in which any notes can be written.

To view records:

1 Switch to the **Company** module. The nominal accounts should be listed. If they are not, click the **Nominal Ledger** link.

2 Double-click on a single record to display it in the record window.

or

3 Select the records to display and click [Record] .

4 Click on the headings to switch between the tabs.

5 Click [Next] to view the next record.

6 Click [Close] when done.

Budgets

If you want to include budget figures to help in analysing and monitoring your business's performance, they can be written into the Details tab of the Nominal Record window.

The budget data can be compared with the actual figures directly on the Details tab, or visually on the Graphs tab. The system can also produce a budget report, showing how far the actual figures differ from the budget, for the period and for the year to date.

To enter budget data:

1 Open the account in the **Nominal Record** window.

2 Enter a budget figure for each month.

or

3 Enter a figure for the year in the Total row. When you have finished, the system will offer to divide it equally between the months.

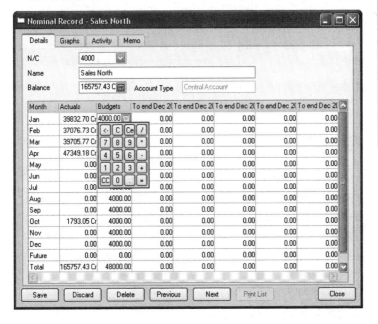

4.3 Chart of Accounts

The Chart of Accounts is used by the Line 50 system when grouping and totalling accounts for calculating the Profit and Loss account (page 173), and when producing the Balance Sheet (page 175). A default chart is created when the software is installed, with a structure to match the company configuration that you selected (see page 53). It can be adjusted to suit the particular needs of your business.

The default layout of the General configuration is summarized below. Accounts are grouped into *categories*, which are then grouped into *category types*. Each category will have a number of standard accounts already in place, and these will normally occupy the first few places in the number sequence. You can add new categories or alter the ranges, to include different accounts.

The **Initial Range** shows the nominal codes currently grouped in each category type. In some cases, there are substantial gaps in a range. With sales, for instance, the main group falls between 4000 and 4299, but there are then sub-ranges for credit charges (4400–4499) and other sales (4900–4999), leaving big gaps where other categories could be inserted if needed. Where a category type has sub-ranges, these are shown below in lighter type.

The **Maximum** shows the highest code that can be included in the category type – the next one is the first in another type.

CATEGORY TYPE	INITIAL RANGE	MAXIMUM
Fixed Assets	0010–0059	0999
Current Assets	1000–1250	1999
Current Liabilities	2100–2299	2299
Long Term Liabilities	2300–2399	2999
Capital & Reserves	3000–3299	3999
Sales	4000–4299	4399
Credit charges	4400–4499	4899
Other sales	4900–4999	
Purchases	5000–5299	5999
Direct Expenses	6000–6299	6999
Miscellaneous Expenses	6900–6999	
Overheads	7000–8299	9997
Suspense & Mispostings	9998–9999	

Note that the Bank accounts (1200–1209) and VAT liability (2200–2209) categories float between the assets and liabilities type depending upon whether they hold credit or debit balances.

To edit the chart of accounts:

1 In the **Company** module, click the ▦ COA button or select the **Chart of Accounts** link.

Alternative charts

You can have several charts of accounts, each presenting the data in different ways, and switch between them as required. To make a chart current, select it and click [Current].

2 Select a **Layout** – there may only be one – and click [Edit].

3 Click on a type to display its categories.

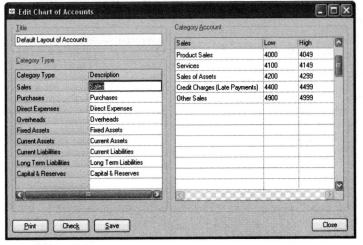

To adjust a range:

4 Type the new **High** code for the **Category,** or click on the down arrow and select the new highest account.

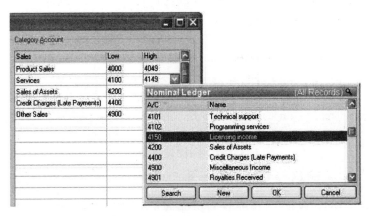

To add a category:

5 Type a suitable name.

6 Type the **Low** and **High** codes, or select them from the lists.

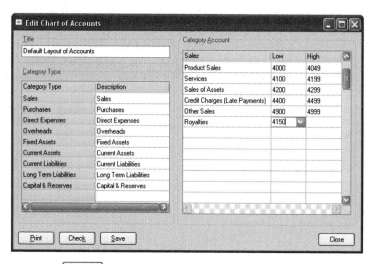

7 Click [Save].

8 Close the **Edit** panel to return to the **Chart of Accounts** panel, and click [Close] to end.

Hand-made charts

If none of the ready-made charts of accounts are close enough to your needs, you can create your own from scratch.

1 Click [Add] to start, and enter a name at the prompt.

2 When the **Edit Chart of Accounts** dialog box opens, the category types will be in place already but they will all be empty. Create your categories, with suitable ranges, for each type.

Check and print

The Edit Chart of Accounts dialog box does not give you a clear overview of the whole chart, and this can lead to errors. You may find it useful – especially if you are creating a new chart or making major changes, to print the chart – click [Print] to get a hard copy. And after making any changes, however small, always click [Check] to get the system to check for overlapping ranges and other errors.

4.4 Editing the Nominal accounts

During installation, Sage Line 50 creates an extensive and well-organized set of nominal accounts, tailored to your type of business (see page 9). This may suit your needs with little or no adjustment, but can be changed easily – unwanted accounts can be deleted or their names edited, or new ones created.

The accounts most likely to need some attention are:

* Stock accounts (numbered from 1000), Sales (4000 onwards) and Purchases (5000 onwards) may well need renaming to suit your types of goods or services.

* Overheads (7000 onwards) should be checked to see that they agree with your categories of expenses.

* You may want to handle computer hardware separately from other office equipment (N/C 0030), as it can be written off in two years, rather than the standard 25% p.a. of other capital equipment. This will require two accounts, which might be named 'Computer Hardware' and 'Computer Depreciation'.

When replacing a default account with your own at the same place in the nominal structure, you can do this by editing the name or by deleting the old one and creating a new one. Do whichever is easier for you.

Some accounts may seem to be unnecessary. Don't delete any unless you are very clear about their intended use and that you do not need them. An empty account takes up a tiny amount of disk space.

Delete with care!

In the Sage system, when a record has been selected it stays selected – so that multiple selections can be made. Just in case some off-screen records are selected, click [Clear] to deselect all records before selecting any deletion.

To edit the accounts:

1 Switch to the **Company** module to display the nominal accounts list.

2 Click on the account(s) you want to change or delete.

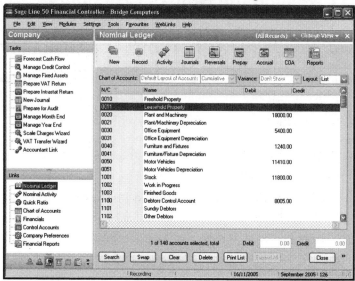

To edit the name:

3 Double-click on the account or right-click on it and select **Edit record...** from the pop-up menu.

4 At the record window, edit the **Name** as required.

5 Click [_Save_] to save the new name.

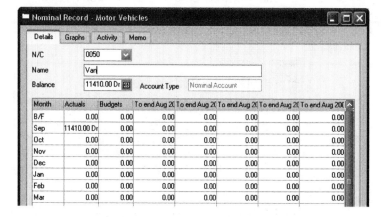

Where did it go?

When you click Save, the details of the account disappear –
don't worry about this! The panel has been cleared ready
for work on another account. This can be selected from the
list that drops down from the N/C (Nominal Code) field.

6   Click [Close] to close the record window and return to the
    main display.

7   Click on the record(s) again, or click [Clear] to deselect.

To delete an account:

8   Make sure that the only accounts selected are those that you
    want to delete.

9   Click [Delete] then confirm at the prompt.

Creating accounts

When creating a new account, the key point to bear in mind is
its location in the chart of accounts. The account must go within
the range of the appropriate type – or just outside if the range
can be extended to include it. If there is an appropriate category
with unused Nominal code, that is the ideal location.

1   Click [New]. This will start the Nominal Record Wizard.

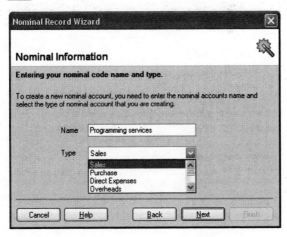

2   At the opening stage, click [Next] to get started.

3   Type a **Name** for the account, then select a **Type** from the list. Click [Next].

4   Select a Category (from the Chart of Accounts – see below). The next available Nominal Code in that category will be allocated to the account. If you do not want the allocated Ref number, change it – but be sure it is in the right range. Click [Next].

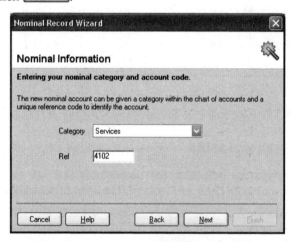

5   You will be asked if you want to enter an opening balance. Select [Yes] if you do, then click [Next].

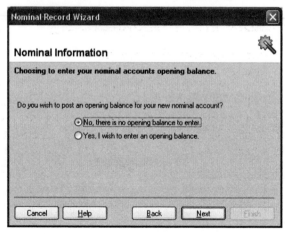

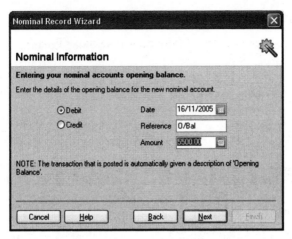

6 Enter the Date and Amount, and check that the default Debit/ Credit selection is appropriate. (See the next section for more on opening balances.) Click [Next].

7 At the final stage, click [Finish] to create the new record.

> ### New accounts and the chart of accounts
> If you create new accounts you may need to adjust the ranges or set up new categories. This can be done before or after creating the accounts.

4.5 Double-entry bookkeeping

When you start to use Line 50 in earnest, you will find that with day-to-day transactions – sales, purchases and payments – you only need to record the details of each transaction once. When you are recording receipt of a payment, for example, you simply tell the system which account the money is going into, which customer has paid which invoice and how much is received. The system then handles the double-entry bookkeeping for you.

It doesn't always work this way. With some transactions you have to make the double entries yourself, and the first time you will come across these is when recording opening balances.

Opening balances

When you transfer to the Sage system, opening balances (O/B) should normally be entered on all accounts where transactions have taken place. In an ongoing business this will probably mean all used accounts, except those of suppliers and customers where debts have been cleared. If the business is just being started up, you will still need to enter opening balances in the Capital and Bank accounts, and perhaps those for property and other assets.

Opening balances may also be needed when you create new accounts. This is less likely with customers and suppliers, where you will normally set up the account with a zero balance before you begin to record your transactions.

Every opening balance must have an equivalent entry in another account – every debit needs a balancing credit, and vice versa. Remember:

+ **Debit**: movement of value into an account.

+ **Credit**: movement of value out of an account.

e.g. when you have bought something, it will be entered as a debit in the apropriate asset, purchase or expense account and a credit in a bank or supplier's account.

The best way to record an opening balance is through the new account wizard or through a record window, as we are doing here. In either case, this will automatically make the balancing entry in the *Suspense* account (N/C 9998), which serves as a temporary home for values. You then have to make a journal entry to move the value from there to its proper home – typically the current or other bank account. This is not difficult, and there are simple ways to ensure that you get it right.

To enter a balance in an existing account:

1 In the appropriate module, locate the record(s) to be edited.

   Double-click – click ▣ Record if several records are selected, to open the record window.

2 Click on the **Balance** field.

3 Set the **Date**.

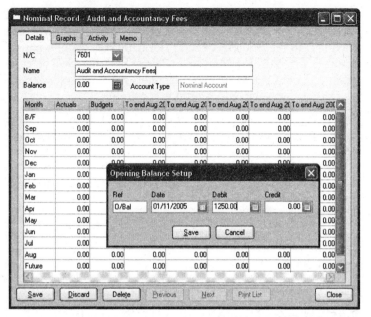

4   Enter the value into the **Debit** or **Credit** field. (Remember, if value is coming into the account, e.g. you're recording the purchase of goods or services, then it's a debit.)

5   Click [Save].

•   If several records have been selected, click [Next] to go to the next, and repeat steps 2 to 5.

6   Click [Close] to close the record window.

7   Back at the Nominal accounts display, scroll to the bottom of the list. You should see that the Suspense account contains an amount equivalent (but opposite) to the opening balance(s). This needs to be moved into the appropriate account(s), and to do that we use journal entries.

4.6 Journal entries

A journal entry is a transfer between Nominal accounts. Typical uses include relocating amounts placed in Suspense, and recording depreciation or the revaluation of stock or other assets.

Making a journal entry is one of the few situations where you have to do the double-entry bookkeeping yourself, rather than leaving it to the system. An entry normally consists of a pair of transactions, one debit, one credit. Sometimes there will be more than two, but the total debits and credits must always balance – you cannot save the entries until it does!

Before you start, make a note of the details of the monies to be moved – the source and target accounts, date, reference and amount.

1 Click 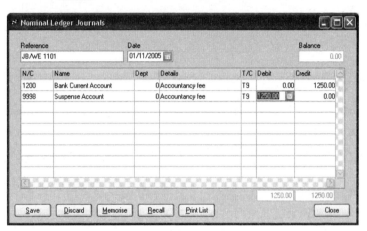 to open the **Nominal Ledger Journals** window.

2 Give a **Reference** to identify the journal.

3 Set the **Date**.

4 Set the N/C number of the Nominal account into which the value will be moved from Suspense.

5 Type the **Details**.

6 Enter the amount in the **Debit** or **Credit** column – this should be the same side as the original Suspense entry.

7 Repeat steps 4 to 6 for the balancing entry to move the amount out of the Suspense account – this will be the opposite debit/credit to the original.

8 If there are several opening balances to correct, repeat steps 2 to 7 for each of them.

9 Click [Save]. If the total debit and credit entries are not the same, you will be told so. You can only save and exit from the journals window when the entries balance.

Reversals

You shouldn't normally need to use these, but it's good to know that the possibility exists. If you discover that a journal entry has been made in error, you can undo it with a reversal.

Before making the reversal, you should ensure the safety of your data. Print out a day book report (see page 92), then run a check on your data and back it up. The system will prompt you to do this.

1 In the Nominal ledger display, click [ ].

2 You will be prompted to print the Day Book report and to backup – do so now if you have not already done so.

3 At the **Transaction Range** dialog box, set the **Range**, the **Date** and/or **Reference** – any or all will filter the display to make it easier to find the transaction you want to reverse.

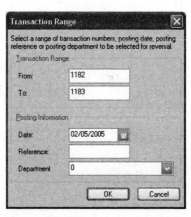

4 Select the pair(s) or transactions to reverse.

5 Click [Reverse].

If the totals of the debit and credit transactions do not balance, you will not be allowed to go any further.

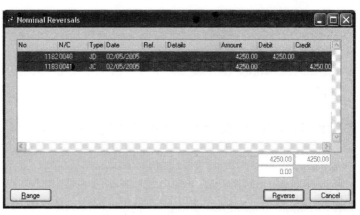

6 The system will generate the reversing transactions and display them. Click [Save] to make the changes.

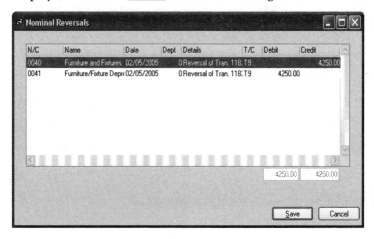

4.7 Activity

If your main interest in the Nominal accounts is in the transactions, you may prefer to view them through the Activity display. The same information is shown as in the Activity tab of the record panel, but you can move more easily between different records here. You can look at the transactions in a preselected set of accounts, and/or select individual accounts once you are in the Activity display window.

Before the window opens, you will have the opportunity to limit the display by setting the number range, types or date limits of the transactions.

1 If you want to look at specific records, select them first.

2 Click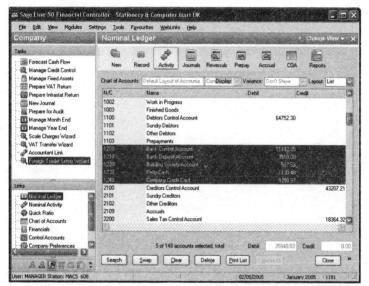

3 Limit the display, if required, by setting the **Transaction Range** or **Type**, or the **Date Range**.

The default date range is 1980 to 2099. It may be quicker to type the dates than set them with the calendar tools!

4 At the Activity window, click ⊞ if you want to see the details of a transaction.

You can select an account here

5 Move through the preselected accounts using the `Next` and `Previous` buttons, or

6 Select an account from the drop-down list.

7 If you want to change the range or types of activity, click `Range` to reopen the **Activity Date Range** dialog box.

8 If you have opened up a lot of transactions, the display can get messy. Click `Tidy List` to restore the summary display.

4.8 Reports

Line 50 has ready-made reports for many purposes. In the Nominal module alone there are nearly 20, grouped into seven sets:

• **Day Books:** lists journal entries and reversals.

• **Departmental:** analyses nominal accounts by departments.

• **Nominal Activity:** shows the transactions in each Nominal account – with or without inactive accounts.

• **Nominal Balances:** lists the balance in each account.

• **Nominal Budgets:** budget reports for the year, half-year or quarter.

- **Nominal Details:** list the Nominal accounts, with or without monthly values. Two of these are in CSV (Comma Separated Values) format, which can be read by most databases and spreadsheets. Use it if you want to process the data further using one of these applications.

- **Nominal Quick Ratio:** lists the assets and liabilities accounts and shows the credit/debit balance (see page 17).

Most reports can list all the accounts or those in a selected range. Depending upon the type of report, this can be based on the nominal code, date, transaction number or department.

1 Click .

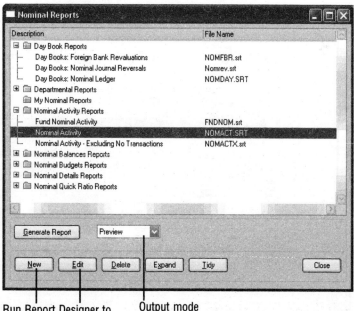

Run Report Designer to   Output mode
create or edit a report

2 Click ⊞ to open the folders and select a layout.

3 Choose the output from the drop-down list – Printer, Preview, File or E-mail.

4 Click [Generate Report] .

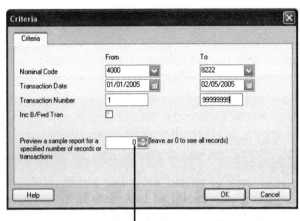

Set a number to preview the report

5 In the **Criteria** dialog box, you can specify a range of nominal codes, transaction dates or numbers.

6 To check that the criteria select the right things, set a number to preview.

7 Click [OK] to generate the report.

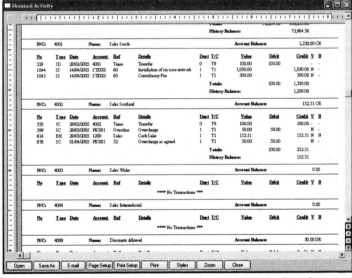

You can print from the Print Preview window – and note the Page Setup and Print Setup buttons here.

Editing a report

Predefined reports can be edited to your requirements. If you worked through the example in Chapter 2 and used the Report Designer to produce a letter from scratch, then you should have no trouble in editing.

1 At the **Nominal Reports** dialog box, select an existing report and click [Edit]. The **Report Designer** window will open.

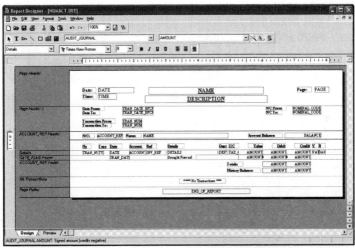

Notice the headings on the left:

Page Header – anything in this area will appear at the top of every page.

Page Header 2 – anything here will appear on the first page only.

ACCOUNT_REF Header – material to appear at the start of each account.

Details – this line is repeated for all transactions in each account.

Footers – printed at the end of each account.

No Transactions – printed if there are no transactions for the account.

Page Footer – appears only on the last page of the report.

2 If you want to add text boxes, variables, lines or boxes to an area, you may need to make more space. Click on the line at the bottom of the area and drag it down. Add your material as shown in Chapter 2 (page 27).

3 When a variable is added, the **Active Complete** dialog box will open. This has three key areas:

To add a label by the variable, select a **Title** option.

If the variable is in a transaction it can have multiple lines. To add a total in the next footer (and in those at the next level of footers), set an option in the **Totals** area.

To format the variable or use it in a function, turn on 'On completion display the Object Properties window'.

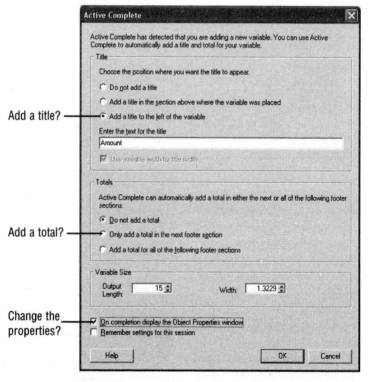

4 In the Object Properties window, the **Function** options can calculate and display the sum, average, minimum, maximum

or count of the copies of the variable. One or other of these may be useful in analysing trading patterns.

5 Type the **Symbols** to use when displaying numbers – note that the default format does not have a thousands separator.

Select a function here   Thousands separator?

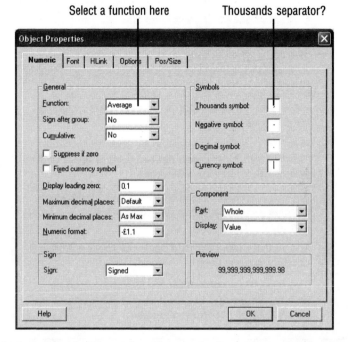

6 Switch to the Font tab to format the font, size and style, then click [OK] when you have done.

7 Preview the report to see the effects of your changes, and don't forget to save it if you may want to reuse it in future.

Print margins

If your printer's page set up does not match the printout's set up, you'll get an error message – use the Fix option, and let the system sort things out!

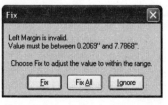

Summary

♦ The Company module covers most of the activities relating to Nominal accounts.

♦ The basic Nominal accounts have been created for you. Unwanted ones can be deleted and new ones created to suit your business.

♦ The Chart of Accounts creates the structure for calculating the Profit and Loss account and Balance Sheet.

♦ When you set up accounts, you can enter opening balances at the time.

♦ If wanted, budget figures can be entered for each month in Nominal accounts. Comparing these with actual figures can be instructive.

♦ Journal entries are used to transfer value between Nominal accounts. Recording depreciation is a typical use for them.

♦ The Activity tab offers the best way to view Nominal account transactions.

♦ The reports available from the Company module include simple and grouped lists of transactions and summaries of account balances.

05 customers and suppliers

In this chapter you will learn:

- how to create records for customers and suppliers
- about viewing and editing records
- how to search for records
- about printouts

5.1 New records

In the Line 50 systems, customers and suppliers are handled in almost identical ways, as you might expect – it is the same trading relationship, but viewed from opposite ends. The examples in this chapter are drawn from the Customers module, but – with rare exceptions – could have come from the Suppliers.

Accounts can be set up from the **New** button in the customers/ suppliers list in those windows that handle invoices, receipts and payments – a blank record opens to take the details. However, the simplest way is to use the New Wizard in the Customers and Suppliers modules. This helps to ensure that all essential information is entered, and creates an A/C (account) reference for you.

1 Open the **Customer** module and click $\boxed{\text{New}}$.

2 Click $\boxed{\text{Next}}$ to get started, and $\boxed{\text{Next}}$ after each stage.

3 Enter the **Name**. An **A/C Ref** will be generated – edit this to make it easier to recognize, if necessary.

4 Enter the **Address details**.

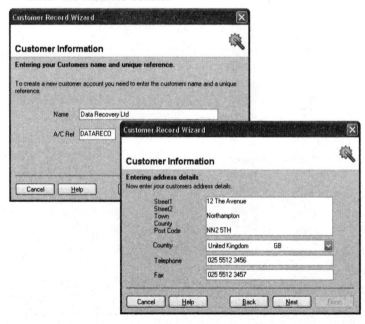

5 Enter the **Contact details** and set the **Account Status** – normally **Open** (active, existing client) or **New**.

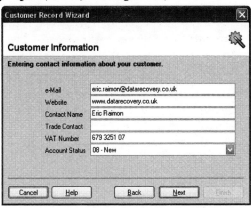

6 At the three **Additional Information** stages, check and adjust the **Credit Limit** and **Terms** as required.

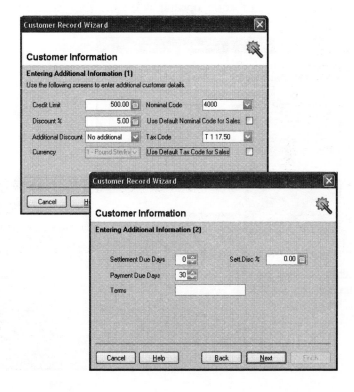

7 If terms have been agreed with the customer, tick the checkbox at the third stage – until this is ticked, you will get a reminder every time you open the account.

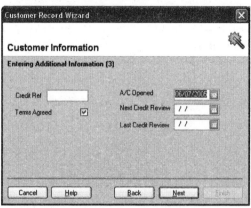

8 If you are bringing an existing customer onto the system, you may need to set the **opening balance**. This is entered as a set of individual transactions.

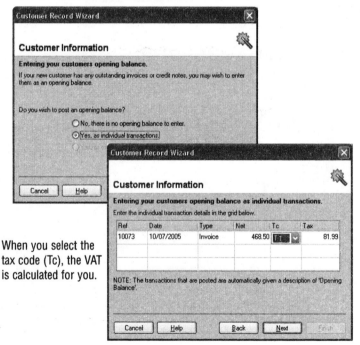

When you select the tax code (Tc), the VAT is calculated for you.

Missing details?

If you do not have all the required information about the new customer, or do not have time to fill it in at that point, you can reopen the record and enter the missing details at any time.

5.2 Viewing and editing records

The record displays for customers and suppliers show not simply their contact details and terms of trade, but also the flow of business to date and the current state of their accounts.

- You can edit the information on the Details, Defaults, Credit Control, Contacts and Memo tabs. The details on the other tabs can only be viewed and not edited.

1 Double-click on the record you want to view or edit

or

2 Select several records and click

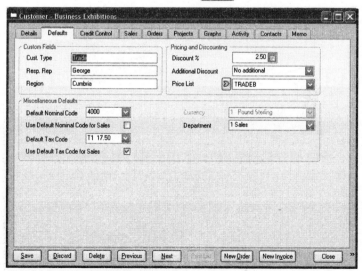

The Previous and Next buttons are only available if several records were selected before opening the window.

The record window buttons

- **Save** writes any changes into the file.

- **Discard** restores the record to how it was before the changes.

- **Delete** deletes the whole **record,** not a transaction. To delete a transaction, use the Corrections routine (see page 34).

- **Previous** opens the next selected record above in the list.

- **Next** opens the next selected record below in the list.

- **New Order** opens the sales order window (see page 129).

- **New Invoice** opens the Invoicing window (see page 116).

- **Close** closes the record window.

Viewing sales activity

You can view the trading activity with your customers in five different ways.

- On the **Sales** tab, you can see a summary of the invoices, credits, balances and receipts for each month, and the details behind each of these figures can be displayed if required.

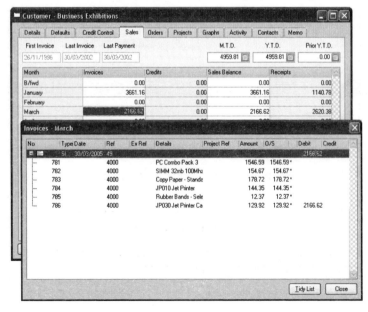

Double-click on a cell to display its details window, then click on ⊞ to open up any item. Click [Close] to return to the main display.

* On the **Orders** tab you can see the status of current and recent orders.

* If you organize and invoice any of your sales through projects, current and recent ones are listed on the **Projects** tab.

* The **Activity** tab lists all the transactions to date, back to the point when the audit trail was last cleared (see page 168). A busy account can produce a long list of transactions. If you don't want to struggle through the list, use the **Range** button to restrict the display to a selected set of transactions.

    Click ⊞ to see the details of an item, and [Tidy List] to close up all expanded items.

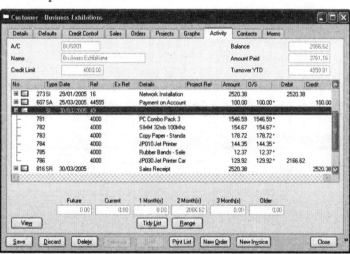

* The **Graphs** tab is perhaps the most complex. It deserves a closer look.

***

Credit control

We'll come back to the record window and look at the Credit Control tab in Chapter 7, Credit Control.

Graphs

Graphs can help to show underlying trends that are not immediately visible from the raw data. With the right sort of graph – bar chart, pie chart, line, scatter or Hi-Lo graph – presented in the right way, you can see relationships and changes over time, much more clearly than you can by poring over sets of numbers. On the other hand, you can spend an awful lot of time trying out different display modes and tweaking the layout and design – and not have much to show for it at the end of the day.

I suspect that, in most firms, the trading patterns with their regular customers/suppliers follow fairly simple trends or seasonal fluctuations, which will show up on simple line, area or bar chart, and little that is useful will come out of any of the more esoteric display modes.

1 Switch to the **Graphs** tab.

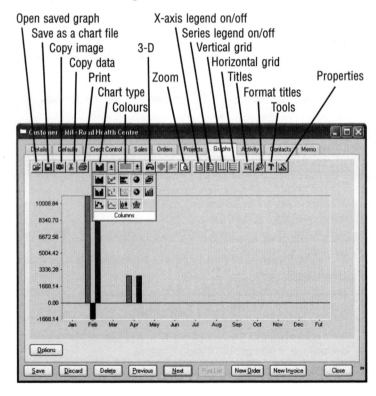

2 Select a **type**.

3 Experiment with the tools to see what they do and find settings that you like.

and/or

4 Click 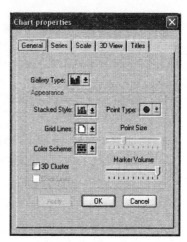 to open the **Properties** dialog box and set the options there.

Play and learn!

If you want to use the graphs productively, spend an hour one day playing with the settings until you are happy with them – then leave them alone. These settings will become the defaults for all future graphs.

Copying graph data

There are two ways in which the graph can be copied and then pasted into another application.

• The **Copy** data tool ✂ copies the figures on which the graph is based to the Clipboard as text. They can then be pasted into a word-processor or spreadsheet. Try not to be confused by the fact that the icon is the one used in other Windows applications for the **Cut** operation!

• The **Copy** image tool 📷 captures the graph as a picture. It can then be pasted into a graphics application, or to a word-processor that can handle images.

5.3 Searching

If you only have a few customers and suppliers, and are reasonably familiar with the state of their accounts, it's no great bother to run through the list selecting them individually when you want to examine or process them. Once you get beyond a few, it's worth learning how to use the Search routine.

By specifying criteria, you can pick out those accounts where the values in a field match a given value. For example:

♦ the customers in a town,

♦ the suppliers whose invoices are due,

♦ trading partners where the annual turnover is over £10,000 or those below £500.

Conditions can be set on as many fields as necessary, to select very specific sets of records. Conditions can be joined by **And**, if both must apply, or **Or**, where records are selected if either or both conditions apply.

The example here is from the Customer module, but the Search routine is used in the same way in all modules.

1 Click [Search].

2 In the **Join** column, select *Where*.

3 Click into the **Field** column and select a field from the list.

4 Click into the **Condition** column and select one.

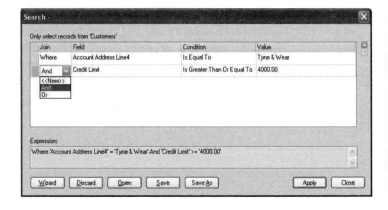

5 Type the **Value**.

6 If you want to set another condition, click into the Join box of the next line and select **And** or **Or**, then work through steps 3 to 5 again.

7 Click [Apply], then [Close].

• The customer list will now only display those records that match the criteria.

8 To display all the records again, reopen the **Search** dialog box and click [Discard], then [Apply] and [Close].

The search wizard

If you prefer, you can set up the search through a wizard. The results are exactly the same – it just walks you through the steps given above. Click [Wizard] to start.

5.4 Customer reports

There are twelve sets of reports that can be obtained from the Customer module.

- The **Customer Details** and **Sales Contacts** reports are useful practical summaries, while the **Top Customer** reports highlight the ones to look after.

- The **Customer Activity, Daily Transaction, Day Book, Departmental** and **EC Sales** reports provide a range of ways to view and analyse your trading patterns.

We'll come back to the **Customer Invoice** reports in Chapter 6 and the **Aged Debtor** and **Credit control** reports in Chapter 7.

To produce a report:

1 Click 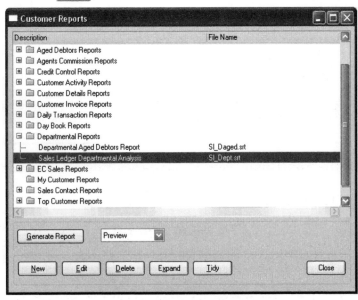 to open the **Customer Reports** dialog box.

2 Click ⊞ to open the folders and select a report layout.

3 Choose the output: Printer, Preview, File or E-mail.

4 Click **Generate Report**.

5   In the **Criteria** dialog box, you can define a range of accounts. You may also be able to set a range of dates, transaction numbers and/or nominal codes, depending upon the report.

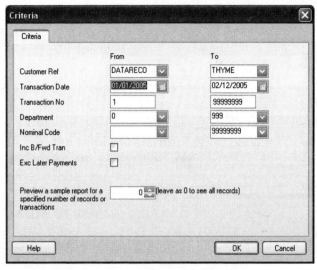

Criteria		
	From	To
Customer Ref	DATARECO	THYME
Transaction Date	01/01/2005	02/12/2005
Transaction No	1	99999999
Department	0	999
Nominal Code		99999999
Inc B/Fwd Tran	☐	
Exc Later Payments	☐	
Preview a sample report for a specified number of records or transactions	0 (leave as 0 to see all records)	
Help		OK Cancel

6   To check a sample, set a number to preview.

7   Click [OK] to generate the report.

If no report meets your requirements, you can edit an existing one, or create one from scratch (see section 2.11, page 43).

5.5 Labels, letters and statements

Statements

In addition to reports, the Customers and Suppliers modules also have a selection of ready-made labels, letters and statements, some designed for output onto plain paper, others onto Sage stationery. Here's how statements can be produced:

1   Select the customer(s) to whom you want to send the statements. (If you want to send them to all customers or to a continuous set from the customer list, do not select any.)

2   Click [Statement].

3 Select the layout – and note that there are different sizes of paper as well as styles of statement.

4 Choose the output: Printer, Preview, File or E-mail.

5 Select the output mode and click [Generate Report].

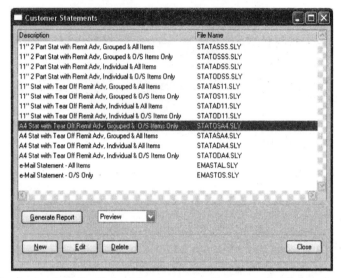

6 At the **Criteria** dialog box, leave the **Customer Ref** fields alone if you selected accounts in step 1. Set a range of **Transaction Dates** if this will be useful, or leave at the defaults to include all current transactions.

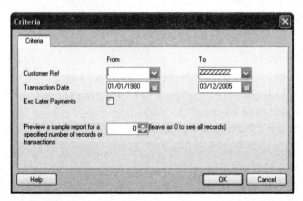

7 Click [OK] to generate the report.

Labels

With labels, the procedure is the same, but you will probably need to change the Page Setup to suit your labels. Line 50 knows some standard labels, and you can easily define your own.

1 Select the customer(s), if appropriate, then click 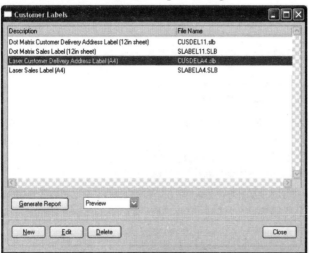.

2 Select the layout – sales or delivery, for 12" or A4 sheets.

3 Click **Edit** to take it into Report Designer.

4 Open the **File** menu and select **Page Setup**.

5 At the **Page Setup** dialog box, first select the **Printer type**, then pick a **Label type** from the list.

6 If you want to check or change the margins and/ or size, click **Modify**.

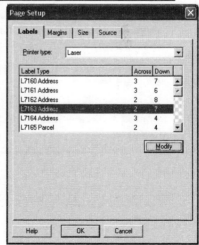

7 After editing, save the design and close Report Designer.

8 Back at the **Labels** dialog box, select the output mode and click [Generate Report], then continue as for statements.

Supplier printouts

The Supplier module has an almost identical range of reports, letters and labels – though no statements, of course – as the Customer module.

Summary

* New customer and supplier accounts are easily set up using the Wizard.

* Records can be viewed and edited by selecting them from the list in the module window.

* The current transactions in an account can be examined through the Activity tab.

* The monthly totals through an account can be viewed as graphs, which may help to make trends clearer.

* A Search will let you control which accounts and records are displayed in a module window.

* If invoices and credit notes have been produced manually, and not through the Invoicing window, record them through the Invoices and Credit routines.

* Statements and letters can be easily printed whenever they are needed.

* Most printouts are designed for use with Sage pre-printed stationery. You can edit layouts in the Report Designer.

06

invoices

In this chapter you will learn:

- how to produce invoices
- about credit notes
- how to update ledgers
- about batch invoices
- about recurring invoices

6.1 The Invoicing window

The tools in the Invoicing window can be used to create, edit and print invoices, credit notes, labels and reports, and to post the transactions to the appropriate accounts in the Customers and Nominal ledgers.

Line 50 has different invoice structures for products and services. When creating a product invoice, on each item line you select a product from your stock list and enter how many. The system then fills in the details, unit price and total cost for you. With a service invoice you have to type in the details and work out the costs yourself.

When a sale involves both materials and labour, there are two possible solutions:

♦   Set up labour as a 'Product', with the sales price being the hourly rate. You may need several records for different types of skilled and unskilled labour. The job can then be processed through a product invoice.

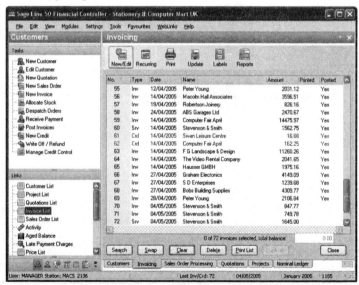

To open the Invoicing window, select Invoice List in the Customer module. The invoices and credit notes listed here can all be reopened for viewing, but they cannot be amended once they have been posted. They are removed when the audit trail is cleared (page 180).

- Include materials in the details of a service invoice. The catches with this are that you will have to calculate material costs, and that product elements will not be posted automatically to the relevant Nominal accounts.

Product invoices

The basic design of an invoice is the same whether it is for a product or a service. There are always:

- Invoice No. – generated automatically.
- Date – also set for you, but can be changed if necessary.
- A/C Ref – selecting this pulls the name and address into the heading area on the top left.
- Order No. – if the customer has given one.
- VAT and the Totals – calculated by the system.

In a Product invoice you also need to specify the items and the quantity of each.

1 Click New/Edit .

2 If *Invoice* is not the default **Type**, select it.

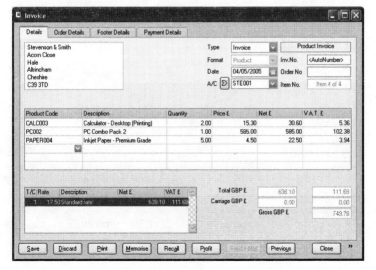

Product Code	Description	Quantity	Price £	Net £	V.A.T. £
CALC003	Calculator - Desktop (Printing)	2.00	15.30	30.60	5.36
PC002	PC Combo Pack 2	1.00	585.00	585.00	102.38
PAPER004	Inkjet Paper - Premium Grade	5.00	4.50	22.50	3.94

T/C	Rate	Description	Net £	VAT £
1	17.50	Standard rate	638.10	111.68

Total GBP £ 638.10   111.68
Carriage GBP £ 0.00   0.00
Gross GBP £ 749.78

3 If *Product* is not the default **Format**, select it.

4 Set the **Date**.

5 Enter an **Order No.** if required.

6 Select the **A/C** code from the list.

7 For a defined product, select its **Code** from the drop-down list; its **Description** and **Price** will be written in for you. For other items, select S1, S2 or S3 and fill in the details yourself.

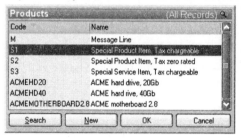

8 Enter the **Quantity**. The **Net** will then be calculated.

9 If you want to edit the description, add a comment, or change the price or other aspect, click the ☑ by the **Description** field to open the **Edit Item Line** dialog box.

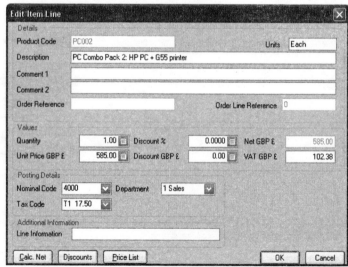

Edit or add details as required – to give a **Discount**, enter either the percentage or the actual amount. Click [OK] when you have done to return to the Invoice window.

10 Repeat steps 7 to 9 for each item. If the running total triggers a new discount level, you will be alerted.

11 Click [Save].

12 Repeat steps 2 to 8 for all invoices, then click [Close].

Further details

Many invoices can be completed simply using the top panel. The other panels allow you to add or adjust the details.

* Use the **Order Details** panel to change the delivery address or contact details from the defaults, or to add any notes.

* Use the **Footer Details** panel to add a carriage charge, or alter the default charge, or to adjust discounts and terms.

* If a payment has been received, this can be recorded on the **Payment Details** tab. The money can be allocated to that invoice, or as a general payment to the account.

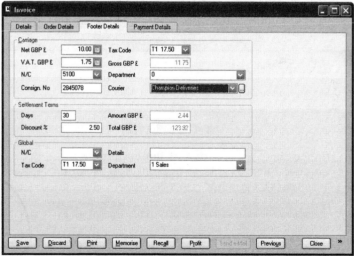

If you use couriers who offer parcel tracking through their websites, add their names and site details to the Couriers list – use Settings > Internet Resources to reach this list.

To change the carriage and terms:

1 Switch to the **Footer Details** panel.

2 Enter the **Carriage** details – costs, codes and courier if used.

3 Adjust the **Terms** as needed.

To record payments:

1 Switch to the **Payment Details** panel.

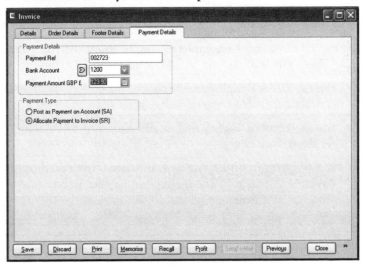

2 Enter the **Ref** and **Amount**.

3 Set any payment to the **account** or the **invoice**.

Is it worth it?

Notice the [Profit] button at the bottom of the Invoice window. Click on this to find out how much profit the business will make from the sale.

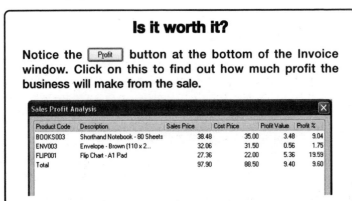

Product Code	Description	Sales Price	Cost Price	Profit Value	Profit %
BOOKS003	Shorthand Notebook - 80 Sheets	38.48	35.00	3.48	9.04
ENV003	Envelope - Brown (110 x 2...	32.06	31.50	0.56	1.75
FLIP001	Flip Chart - A1 Pad	27.36	22.00	5.36	19.59
Total		97.90	88.50	9.40	9.60

Service invoices

1 Begin as for a product invoice (page 116), but select *Service* as the **Format**.

2 Type the **Details**.

3 Enter the **Amount**.

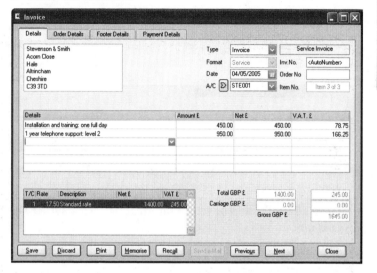

4 To add an item, press **[Tab]** or click into the next blank line and repeat steps 2 and 3.

5 Click [Save].

6.2 Credit notes

Credit notes are the mirror image of invoices and produced in exactly the same way. Probably the most important thing with these is to make sure that they match the original invoice. Have prices changed since it was issued? Did you give a discount?

1 Check the details of the items in the original invoice.

2 Begin as for an invoice, but select *Credit* as the **Type**. The **Format** should be *Product* or *Service* to match the invoice.

3 Enter the details and price of the credited item or service.

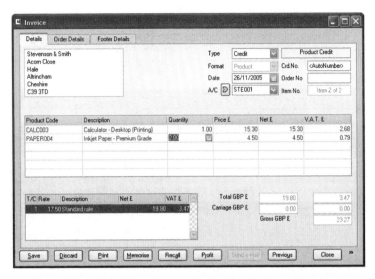

4 Double-click on the Description to open the Edit Item Line
   window if you need to edit any of the details.

5 Enter any collection or return information on the **Order Details** tab.

6 Click [Save].

6.3 Printing invoices

Whether you are printing one invoice or many, the steps are the
same. The difference is in how you start.

* With a single invoice or credit note, it is simplest to start
  from the **Print** button on the **Invoice** window.

* If you are processing a set of invoices, it is more efficient to
  start printing from the main **Invoicing** window.

1 **To print a single invoice:** reopen it if necessary and click
   [Print] at the bottom of the dialog box.

Or

2 **To print several invoices:** select them and click .

3 Pick a layout.

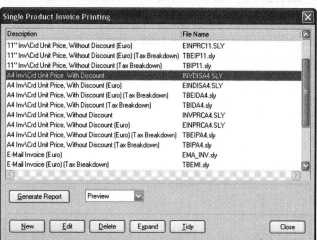

4 Select **Preview** to check the output on screen before printing, or **Print** to print immediately.

5 Click [Generate Report].

A preview of an invoice report designed for pre-printed stationery

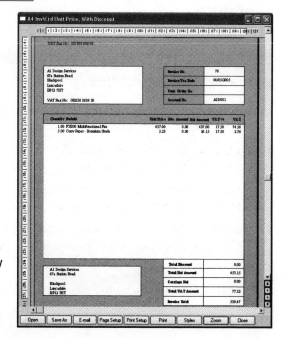

6.4 Updating ledgers

When you create and save an invoice or credit note, its information is stored in your files, but the effect of the transaction on other accounts is not recorded immediately. To 'post' the data to the relevant customers' and nominal accounts, you must use the **Update** button.

The system always shows the transactions it has performed. These can be output to paper or file, if required, or simply viewed on screen.

1 If only certain invoices are to be posted, select them first – otherwise all the unposted invoices will be processed.

2 Click [Update].

3 If a paper copy is needed, select **Printer**; if you need a file copy for future reference select **File**; otherwise select **Preview**.

4 Click [OK].

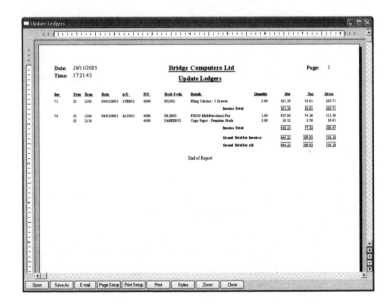

Date:	26/11/2005				**Bridge Computers Ltd**				Page:	1
Time:	17:21:43				**Update Ledgers**					

Inv	Type	Tran	Date	A/C	N/C	Stock Code	Details	Quantity	Net	Tax	Gross
75	SI	1208	04/05/2005	STEI002	4000	FIL002	Filing Cabinet - 5 Drawer	3.00	191.10	32.61	223.71
							Invoice Total		191.10	32.61	223.71
76	SI	1209	04/05/2005	A1D001	4000	FAX003	FX030 Multifunctional Fax	1.00	437.00	74.56	511.56
	SI	1210			4000	PAPER003	Copy Paper - Premium Grade	5.00	16.15	2.76	18.91
							Invoice Total		453.15	77.32	530.47
							Grand Total for Invoices:		644.25	109.93	754.18
							Grand Total for All:		644.25	109.93	754.18

End of Report

Open | Save As | E-mail | Page Setup | Print Setup | Print | Styles | Zoom | Close

6.5 Batch invoices

Invoices and credit notes for your customers are normally dealt with through the Invoicing window, where they can be created, printed and the transactions posted to the ledgers. So, in the Customer module, the batch invoices and credits routines are there to record the transactions when invoices or credit notes have been produced manually. In the Supplier module however, they are the main way to record your transactions.

1 In the **Suppliers** (or **Customers**) window click [Invoice].

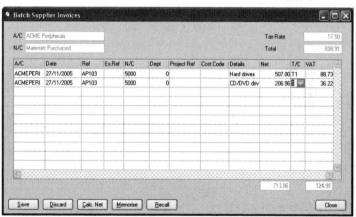

2 Select the account from the **A/C** list.

3 Enter the date and other details.

4 Enter the **Net** amount.

5 If the price is VAT-inclusive, click [Calc. Net].

6 Click [Save].

7 Repeat as needed, then click [Close].

How many lines?

An invoice can be recorded in a single line. If it is for several items and you want to record each separately, use a new line for each, but keep the same Ref code.

Calculating VAT

The system calculates VAT, whether prices are given Net or VAT-inclusive. Prices are always entered into the Net column.

◆ With Net prices, the VAT will appear automatically when you click into the T/C column or into the line below.

◆ With VAT-inclusive prices, click [Calc. Net] and the system will split the total into the Net and VAT elements.

Credit notes

These are handled in almost exactly the same way as invoices. The key point to note is that the reference number here must be that of the invoice against which the credit is being given.

1 Look up the **Reference** number of the invoice in the customer or supplier's **Activity** tab.

2 Click [Credit] in the main **Customers** (or **Suppliers**) window.

3 Complete as for invoices, but with the original **Ref** numbers.

6.6 Recurring invoices

* *Only available in Accountant Plus and Financial Controller.*

If you are issuing an invoice regularly to a customer, e.g. for rent, a maintenance contract or a standing order for goods, then this can be automated by setting it up as a recurring invoice. It only takes a moment to do, but it saves you having to generate a new invoice each time – and it helps to ensure that invoices are produced on time.

1 Start as you would with any invoice, filling in all relevant details. (See page 116 for more on invoicing.)

2 When you have finished, return to the **Details** tab, and click the [Memorise] button in the bottom row.

3 At the **Memorise** dialog box, type a reference and description to identify it in the recurring entries list.

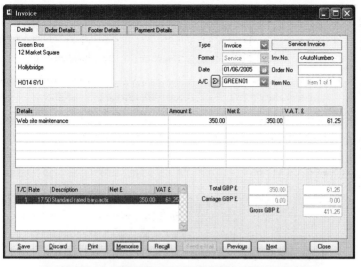

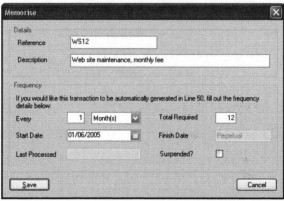

4 In the **Frequency** area, set it to **Every** so many days/months or years, and give a **Start Date.** If only a limited number of invoices are to be issued, e.g. as for an annual contract, then set the **Total Required,** otherwise leave this at 0 for indefinite repetition.

5 Click ⟨ Save ⟩ to return to the **Invoice** window, then save the invoice.

The invoice will be added to the list of recurring items. At the start of each day, Line 50 will check this list and if any are due to be issued, you will be prompted to deal with them.

6 In the **Invoicing** window, click the 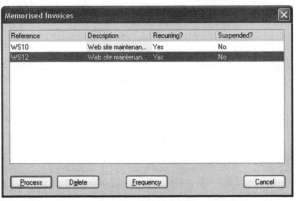 toolbar button.

7 At the **Memorised Invoices** window, click `Process`.

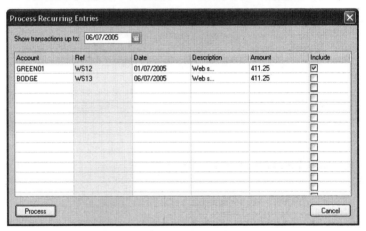

8 Tick the **Include** box for those invoices that you want to generate and click `Process`. You can then update the ledgers and print these as for normal invoices.

Recurring payments in Accountant

The Recurring Entries routine in the Bank module can be used to manage regular payments from customers, though without generating the invoices. See page 155.

6.7 Order processing

The Financial Controller version of Line 50 has sales and order processing routines. Invoices are generated automatically from these when the orders are marked as completed. In addition, sales order processing is linked to stock control, allocating items from stock – if available – against the order and updating those records, and can generate a delivery note when the order is completed.

A sales/purchase order is created in almost exactly the same way as an invoice. Here's the process for a sales order:

1   In the **Customer** module, select the **New Sales Order** task.

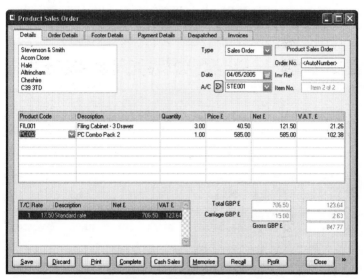

2   If *Sales Order* is not the default **Type**, select it.

3   Set the **Date**.

4   Select the **A/C** code from the list.

5   Select the Product **Code** or select S1, S2 or S3. If necessary enter or edit the description.

6   Enter the **Quantity**. The **Net** will then be calculated.

7   Repeat steps 5 and 6 for each item.

8   If the order is not yet complete, click [Save]. When the goods are ready for despatch, reopen the order and come back to this point.

9   If the order is complete, click [Complete].

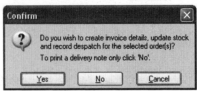

10 At the **Confirm** dialog box, click [Yes] if you want to create the invoice and delivery note, and update the stock. Click [No] to just create the delivery note. This can be printed immediately or left on file for later printing.

Labels

If you want address labels to send out the invoices, there are four ready-made layouts available. Click the Labels toolbar button to start. (See page 113 for more on labels.)

6.8 Reports

You will find five sets of ready-made reports in the Invoicing window.

* The **Invoice Details** reports include *Invoices Not Printed* and *Invoices not Posted* which give lists of those invoices and credit notes awaiting one or other process. There are also reports showing sales by product and by customer.

* The **Invoice Profit** reports set has a variety of itemized and summary profit reports.

* **Quotation** reports are exactly that.

* **Sales by Analysis Code** give several ways to analyse sales.

* **Stock requirements and shortfalls** help you to keep track of stock in relation to sales.

To produce a report:

1 Select the records and click .

2 Click ⊞ to open the folders and select a report layout.

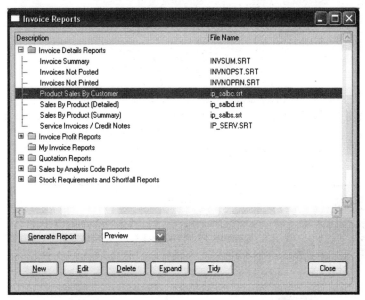

3 Choose the output: Printer, Preview, File or E-mail.

4 Click Generate Report.

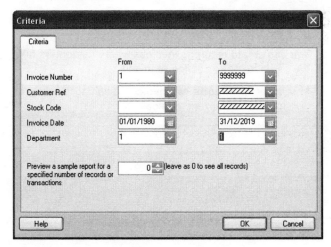

5   In the **Criteria** dialog box, specify a range of invoice numbers and/or dates, customer refs, stock codes or departments as appropriate.

6   To check a sample, set a number to preview.

7   Click [OK] to generate the report.

The reports can, of course, be edited if you want to adapt them to your needs, or you can create your own.

Summary

+ Invoices and credit notes can be produced through the Invoicing window.

+ When creating product invoices, prices are taken from the relevant product records. The details of each product can be adjusted, as necessary.

+ With service invoices, a job can be broken down into several items, each of which can be described over several lines.

+ Credit notes are produced in the same way as invoices. The notes' reference numbers should match those of the original invoice.

+ Each invoice can be printed as it is created, or a selected batch can be printed in one operation later.

+ Transactions are not recorded in the relevant accounts until the Update ledgers routine is run.

+ You can create recurring invoices where customers take the same items or service regularly.

+ The invoicing reports list invoices awaiting printing or updating, or all current invoices.

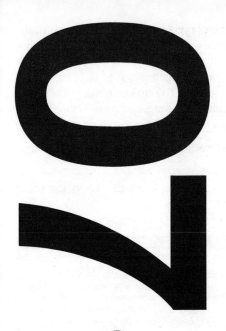

07
credit control

In this chapter you will learn:

- about managing customer credit
- about day sales analysis
- how to record contacts in Line 50
- about aged analysis and write-offs of debts

7.1 Managing customer credit

Good control of your cash flows – in and out of the business – is an essential part of successful management. And to keep control of those flows, you need to be able to find out quickly and easily how much money is owing, for how long, and to and from whom. Line 50's credit control facilities can give you that information.

The key one for inward flows is the **Customer Credit Control** window.

1 Go to the **Customer** module and from the **Tasks** list select **Manage Credit Control**.

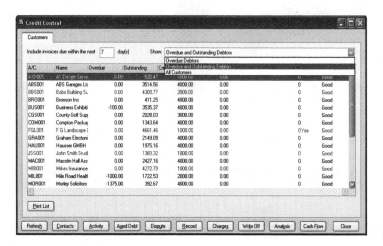

2 In the **Show** field, at the top of the window, select **Overdue**, or **Overdue and Outstanding Debtors**, or **All Customers**.

Sorting

The list can be sorted in order of any column by clicking on the column header; e.g. to sort in ascending order of the amount outstanding:

• Click once on the Outstanding header.

To sort into descending order:

• Click on the header a second time.

Apart from [Refresh], which updates the display with any changes, and the inevitable [Close], all of the other buttons open new windows in which you can view or analyse the credit information in different ways. Four of these can be covered briefly:

[Record] displays the customer's record.

[Activity] displays the trading Activity tab of the selected customer – you can only select one at a time in this window.

[Dispute] is used to record a dispute on a transaction.

[Charges] is used to apply charges on overdue accounts. To be able to do this, you need to set up finance rates in the Terms tab of the Configuration Editor, and turn on Can Charge Credit on your customer records – and agree the terms with your customers!

The other five buttons need rather more discussion.

7.2 Day Sales Analysis

The analysis window shows you how much is outstanding and overdue. You can see this as a graph, if you want an overview of how the business is doing, or in detail.

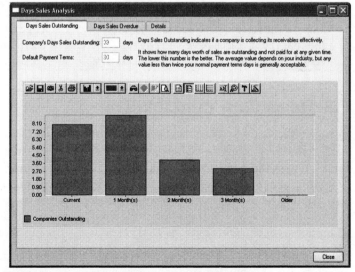

The graphs give you an overview of the payment patterns.

1 Click [Analysis] to open the **Days Sales Analysis** window.

2 Switch to the **Days Sales Outstanding** or **Overdue** tabs to see the graphs.

3 Use the **Details** tab to see exactly how much is owing and for how long.

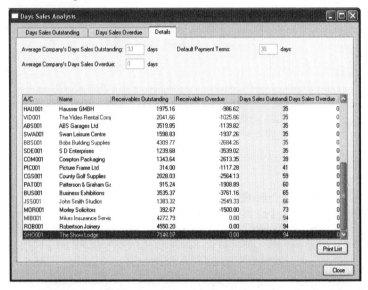

A/C.	Name	Receivables Outstanding	Receivables Overdue	Days Sales Outstandi	Days Sales Overdue
HAU001	Hausser GMBH	1975.16	-986.62	35	0
VID001	The Video Rental Com	2041.66	-1025.86	35	0
ABS001	ABS Garages Ltd	3519.85	-1139.82	35	0
SWA001	Swan Leisure Centre	1598.83	-1937.26	35	0
BBS001	Bobs Building Supplies	4309.77	-2684.26	35	0
SDE001	S D Enterprises	1239.68	-3539.02	35	0
COM001	Compton Packaging	1343.64	-2613.35	39	0
PIC001	Picture Frame Ltd	314.00	-1117.28	41	0
CGS001	County Golf Supplies	2028.03	-2564.13	59	0
PAT001	Patterson & Graham Ga	915.24	-1908.89	60	0
BUS001	Business Exhibitions	3535.37	-3761.16	65	0
JSS001	John Smith Studios	1383.32	-2549.33	66	0
MOR001	Morley Solicitors	392.67	-1500.00	73	0
MIB001	Mikes Insurance Servic	4272.79	0.00	94	0
ROB001	Robertson Joinery	4550.20	0.00	94	0
SHO001	The Show Lodge	7148.07	0.00	94	0

Average Company's Days Sales Outstanding: 33 days   Default Payment Terms: 30 days

Average Company's Days Sales Overdue: 0 days

[Print List]

[Close]

4 Click on the headings to sort by the amount or the length of time that the invoices have been owing. This can be useful in deciding where to concentrate your efforts.

7.3 Recording contacts

Anyone who runs a business dealing mainly with credit customers – especially if it is a smaller business and the customers are larger firms – knows the difficulty of finding the right balance between prompting the slower payers with sufficient vigour to be taken seriously and harrassing them to the point where you lose future custom. Life is simpler in those countries which have strict limits on how quickly debts must be paid!

The contact history routine allows you to keep a track on when a customer was contacted, and what was agreed.

1 Select the customer.

2 Click [Contacts] to open the first **Contact History** window –
   this shows any contacts made to date. Click [New] to record
   a new contact.

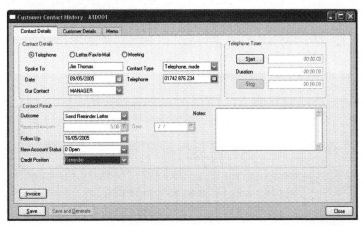

3 In the **Contact Details** section at the top, select **Telephone**,
   Letter/Fax/e-Mail or **Meeting**. The details will vary accord-
   ing to the nature of the contact, and for telephone calls the
   Timer display will appear, so that you can time its duration.

4 Fill in the details, and the outcome or results.

5 Click [Save] to store the details and return to the History
   display.

7.4 Cash Flow

The Cash Flow window shows the state of the bank account(s)
if payments are made and received on their forecast dates. When
using this, it is important to remember that it is based on guess-
work – when figures are shown to the exact penny it is all too
easy to think that they are exact.

1 Click [Cash Flow] to open the **Cash Flow** window.

2 In the **A/C** area at the top right, tick the checkboxes for those
   accounts that you want to include in the running balance.

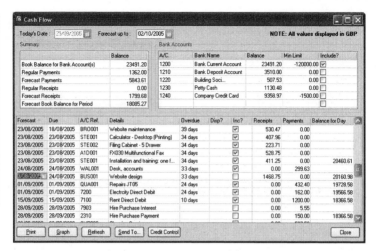

3 To change a forecast date, click on it to make the calendar icon appear, and use that to set the date.

4 Tick the **Inc?** checkbox to include the receipt or payment in the running balance – or clear the checkbox if you decide that the money will not come in or go out on that day.

5 After making any changes, click [Refresh] to update the screen display.

The [Send To...] button will export the data to Excel if you want to process it further.

7.5 Aged analysis

The Aged Analysis window shows the amounts owing by the selected customers (or to the selected suppliers) in each ageing period.

The analysis can be started from the Credit Control window or from the toolbars in the Customer or Supplier windows. Use the latter approach if you want to examine a number of accounts at the same time.

1 In the **Credit Control** window, select the account and click [Aged Debt].

or

2 In the Customers/Suppliers window, select the accounts to include and click 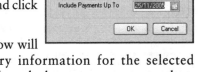.

3 Set the report date and the date to include payments to, and click OK.

Aged Balances Date Defaults		
Enter Range		
Aged Balance Report Date	25/11/2005	
Include Payments Up To	25/11/2005	
	OK	Cancel

4 The **Aged Balances** window will open, showing summary information for the selected account(s). Note the totals at the bottom – you can see these as a graph on the **Graph** tab.

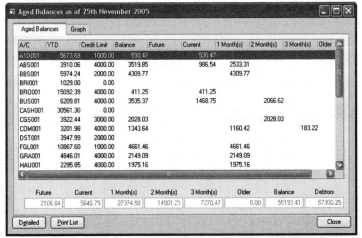

A/C	YTD	Credit Limit	Balance	Future	Current	1 Month(s)	2 Month(s)	3 Month(s)	Older
A1D001	5673.63	1000.00	530.47		530.47				
ABS001	3910.06	4000.00	3519.85		986.54	2533.31			
BBS001	5974.24	2000.00	4309.77			4309.77			
BRI001	1029.00	0.00							
BRO001	15092.39	4000.00	411.25		411.25				
BUS001	6209.81	4000.00	3535.37		1468.75		2066.62		
CASH001	30561.30	0.00							
CGS001	3922.44	3000.00	2028.03				2028.03		
COM001	3201.98	4000.00	1343.64			1160.42		183.22	
DST001	3947.99	2000.00							
FGL001	10867.60	1000.00	4661.46			4661.46			
GRA001	4846.01	4000.00	2149.09			2149.09			
HAU001	2295.85	4000.00	1975.16			1975.16			

Future	Current	1 Month(s)	2 Month(s)	3 Month(s)	Older	Balance	Debtors
2106.84	5646.75	27374.93	14901.21	7270.47	0.00	55193.41	57300.25

Detailed | Print List | Close

5 For a closer look at an account, double-click on it to display it in the **Detailed Aged Analysis** window.

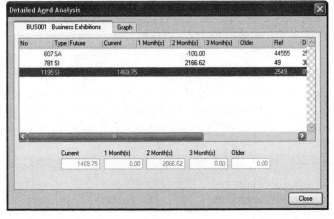

Detailed Aged Analysis

BUS001 Business Exhibitions | Graph

No	Type	Future	Current	1 Month(s)	2 Month(s)	3 Month(s)	Older	Ref	D
607	SA				-100.00			44555	2
781	SI				2166.62			49	3
1195	SI		1468.75					2549	3

Current	1 Month(s)	2 Month(s)	3 Month(s)	Older
1468.75	0.00	2066.62	0.00	0.00

Close

7.6 Write-offs

Write offs, refunds and returns are all handled by a wizard that is started from the [Write Off] button in the Credit Control window. Here's how low value write-offs are managed – the other types and refunds and returns are similarly straightforward.

1 In the **Credit Control** window, click [Write Off].

2 At the **Write Off, Refunds and Returns Wizard,** select **Write off Customer Transactions below a value.** Click [Next].

3 Enter the maxim value to write off. Click [Next].

4 Any transactions below the limit will be listed. Make sure that only those that you really want to write off are selected.

5 Set the date and add a reference for the operation.

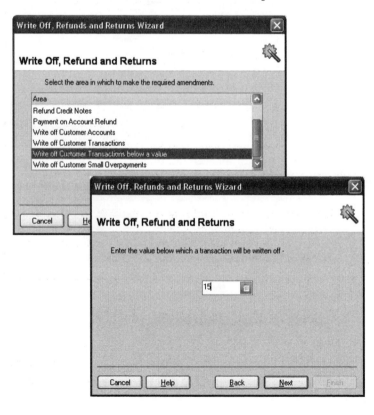

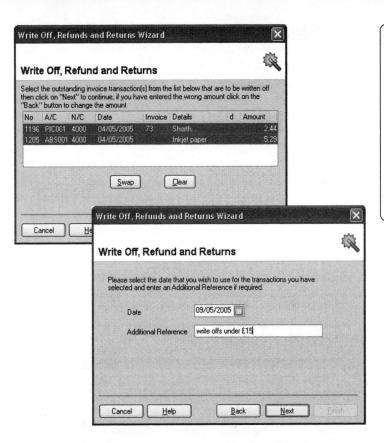

VAT cash accounting?

Note that the use of the Write off, Refunds and Returns Wizard is not recommend where the firm uses VAT cash accounting as the transactions are posted with a tax code that would exclude them from the VAT return.

7.7 Managing supplier credit

The Credit Control window looks almost the same when opened from the Suppliers area. Look a little closer and you will see that a couple of buttons are missing and we've a new one – Payments.

If you want to pay several suppliers at the same time, it is simpler to use this routine than the Pay Supplier routine in the Bank module (see page 152).

1 In the Credit Control window, click [Payments].

2 Decide how much money you have available and enter this in the **Funds for Payment** field at the top left.

   You can allocate funds to suppliers in two ways. Either:

3 Click [Suggest]. The funds will be allocated from the top down – paying each supplier in full, as far as possible then allocating a partial payment with any remaining cash.

or

4 Allocate the funds by typing in values or using the calculator – the latter being very handy if you want to work out how much is left after earlier allocations. Note that the system does not work this out for you. The **Paid** and **Remaining** values are only updated after you have made the payment – not simply allocated an amount.

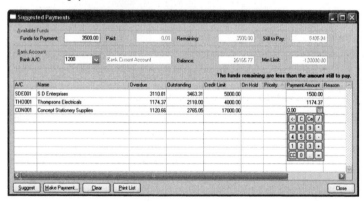

5 When you have worked out how much to pay each, select a supplier and click [Make Payment...].

6 The **Supplier Payment** window will open, showing the outstanding transactions. You can pay all or a selection of these.

7 To pay a selected transaction, click on it and enter the amount to pay or click [Pay in Full] to pay the total amount.

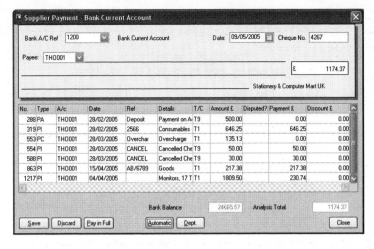

8   To pay all transactions fully, click <u>Automatic</u>. Note that if
    insuffient funds were allocated to this supplier at the earlier
    stage, the transactions will be paid from the top down until
    nothing is left.

9   Click <u>Save</u> to record the payments in your files, then <u>Close</u>
    to return to the **Suggested Payments** window to process the
    next supplier.

Cheque printing

**Accountant Plus and Financial Controller can print your
cheques for you – see page 159.**

Summary

*   The credit control facilities will show you clearly who owes you money, how much and for how long.

*   Keeping records of your contacts with customers is an essential part of good credit control management.

*   The Cash Flow window can help to predict the state of your bank account, if used thoughtfully.

*   The aged analysis facility will show what bills are overdue and by how long.

*   There's a wizard to help you manage write-offs, refunds and returns.

*   The routines for managing supplier credit includes one for allocating funds against several invoices in one batch.

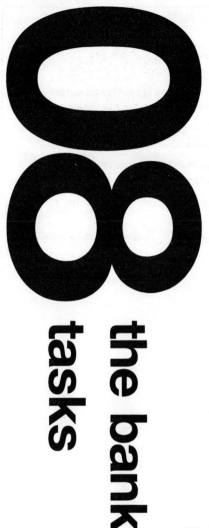

08

the bank tasks

In this chapter you will learn:

- about the Bank tasks and tools
- about reconciliation
- how to record payments made and received
- how to print cheques and remittance advice slips

8.1 The Bank module

This module gives you a different view of, and more ways of working with, those Nominal accounts which are used for the payment and receipt of money. The routines here can be used to make and record payments to suppliers, record receipts from customers, set up recurring payments, move money between accounts, reconcile your accounts with the bank statements and similar activities.

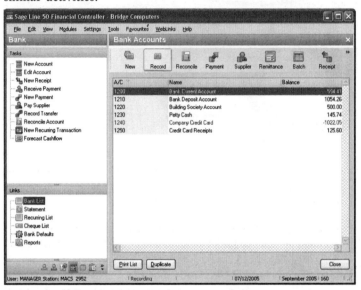

Note that in the Bank List, you can only select one account at a time – and for some operations, you don't need to select any.

To examine a Bank account:

1 ⌐ Select an account.

2 Click ⌐Record⌐.

3 Go to the **Bank Details** and **Contact** tabs to see or update contact information for the bank.

4 Go to the **Activity** tab to examine transactions that have passed through that account.

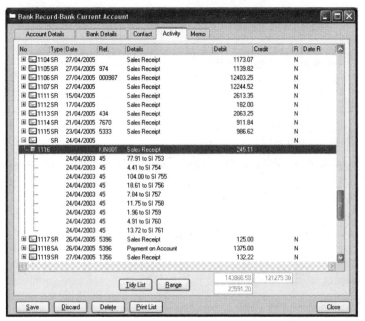

No	Type	Date	Ref.	Details	Debit	Credit	R	Date R
⊞ 1104	SR	27/04/2005		Sales Receipt	1173.07		N	
⊞ 1105	SR	27/04/2005	974	Sales Receipt	1139.82		N	
⊞ 1106	SR	27/04/2005	000987	Sales Receipt	12403.25		N	
⊞ 1107	SR	27/04/2005		Sales Receipt	12244.52		N	
⊞ 1111	SR	15/04/2005		Sales Receipt	2613.35		N	
⊞ 1112	SR	17/04/2005		Sales Receipt	182.00		N	
⊞ 1113	SR	21/04/2005	434	Sales Receipt	2063.25		N	
⊞ 1114	SR	21/04/2005	7670	Sales Receipt	911.84		N	
⊞ 1115	SR	23/04/2005	5333	Sales Receipt	986.62		N	
⊟	SR	24/04/2005					N	
⊟ 1116			KIN001	Sales Receipt	245.11			
		24/04/2003	45	77.91 to SI 753				
		24/04/2003	45	4.41 to SI 754				
		24/04/2003	45	104.00 to SI 755				
		24/04/2003	45	18.61 to SI 756				
		24/04/2003	45	7.84 to SI 757				
		24/04/2003	45	11.75 to SI 758				
		24/04/2003	45	1.96 to SI 759				
		24/04/2003	45	4.91 to SI 760				
		24/04/2003	45	13.72 to SI 761				
⊞ 1117	SR	26/04/2005	5396	Sales Receipt	125.00		N	
⊞ 1118	SA	26/04/2005	5396	Payment on Account	1375.00		N	
⊞ 1119	SR	27/04/2005	1356	Sales Receipt	132.22		N	

[Tidy List] [Range]   143966.58 | 121275.38
22591.20

[Save] [Discard] [Delete] [Print List]   [Close]

5 Click ⊞ if you want to see the details of any transaction, e.g. to see which invoices are covered by a sales receipt.

6 Click [Range] if you want to view only a limited set of transactions. At the **Defaults** dialog box you can set the range of numbers, and/or the type to display, and/or the date range.

The initial date range is from 01/01/1980 to 31/12/2099! Clearly your records won't cover that range, and it is a fiddly job resetting the calendar to more realistic limits.

Defaults

Transaction Range
From: 1
To: 1224

Transaction Type
Type to Display: SR - Sales Receipts
Outstanding Transactions Only? ☐

Date Range
From: 01/01/2005
To: 30/05/2005

[OK] [Cancel]

Bank accounts in the Nominal module

The Bank accounts can also be opened through the Nominal module, and you must use this to reach the graphs and the budgetting facilities.

8.2 Reconciliation

Reconciliation is one of those chores that cannot be automated fully, but at least the Line 50 system makes it straightforward. As you mark items that match entries in your bank statement, the system calculates and displays the difference between your recorded end balance and that of the bank statement. If they do not match after you have worked through the list, you can see how much it is adrift and will probably have a clear idea of the source of the problem.

1 Select an account.

2 Click [Reconcile] on the Bank Accounts toolbar.

3 At the **Statement Summary** dialog box, enter the **Ending Balance** from your bank statement – the balance in your Line 50 Bank account will have been written in as the default.

4 If the statement shows interest earned or charges, enter the amounts and select the appropriate N/C codes.

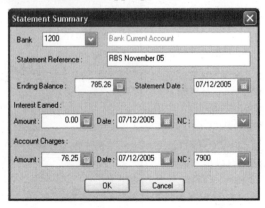

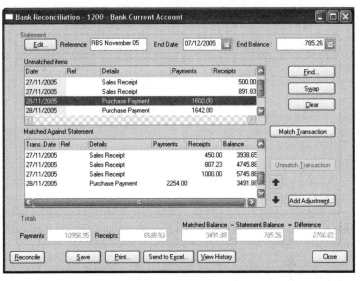

5   Click [OK] to open the **Bank Reconciliation** window.

6   Work through the list. Select each item in the **Unmatched** list
    in turn. If you can match it with the bank statement, mark it
    off on the statement and click [Match Transaction] to move the item
    to the **Matched** list.

7   If you do not have the time or the information to complete
    the reconciliation, you can click [Save] to save the work
    done so far, then restart the process later using the saved data.

8   When all the items have been reconciled, if the **Difference** is
    not 0.00, you need to track down the missing transactions,
    or identify the ones entered incorrectly. When you have found
    them, click [Add Adjustment] and enter its details.

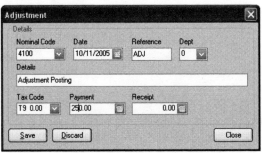

9　When you are done, click ⎡ Reconcile ⎤.

10 If there is a difference between your Bank account and the statement amount, you can add an adjustment at this point, or choose to ignore the difference.

8.3 Payments and receipts

There are five routines here. New Payments and New Receipts are designed to handle cash transactions – and these can be done in batches if required. The Pay Supplier and Receive Payment are there to record settlement of credit transactions. (These can also be accessed through the Customer and Supplier modules). Finally, the Batch routine offers a convenient way to deal with payments for credit purchases, in batches.

The example here is from the **New Payment** routine, but the same method is used to process cash receipts.

1　Select a Bank account.

2　Click ⎡ 📄 Payment ⎤ or select the **New Payment** task.

3　Set the **Date** and give a **Ref** code if required.

4　Select the **N/C** code of the account for the goods or service.

5　Enter the **Details** of the sale or purchase.

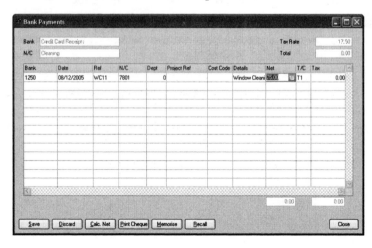

6 Enter the amount into the **Net** box – if this is VAT-inclusive, click [Calc. Net] to split it into Net and VAT.

7 If you are using Accountant Plus or Financial Controller, and want to use the cheque printing facilities, click [Print Cheque].

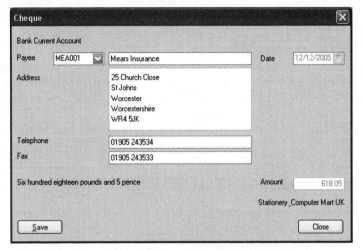

Select the Payee from the suppliers list, or type in the name and address, then click [Save]. The details will be added to the cheque list for later printing (see page 159).

8 Repeat for any other items.

9 Click [Save].

8.4 Receive Payment

Use this routine for recording monies received from credit customers, one at a time. The Receive Payment window shows the outstanding invoices for the selected customer. Receipts can be either allocated to specific invoices, or automatically set against invoices in reference number (not *date*) order.

1 Select the Bank account to take the money.

2 Click [Customer] or select the **Receive Payment** task.

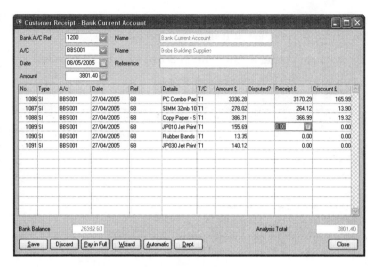

3 Select the customer from the **A/C** list.

4 Set the **Date** and enter the **Ref**.

5 Enter the **Amount** of the payment.

6 Click Automatic to set this against invoices. The monies will be allocated from the top down until the amount is exhausted, paying each in full, and the last one whatever is left.

or

7 Select an invoice and enter an amount or click Pay in Full. If there is a discount, enter this in the end column. Repeat as required.

8 Click Save.

9 Go back to step 3 for the next customer, or click Close.

8.5 Supplier Payments

The Receive Payment and Pay Supplier routines are virtually identical in the way that they work, though they look a little different as the Pay Supplier window has a cheque display at the top. (And if you have Accountant Plus or Financial Controller, then the systems will write your cheques for you, as well as showing you how they should look!)

As you enter amounts against invoices, the system calculates the total and shows it in words and figures in the 'cheque' at the top.

1 Select the account from which the payment will be made.

2 Click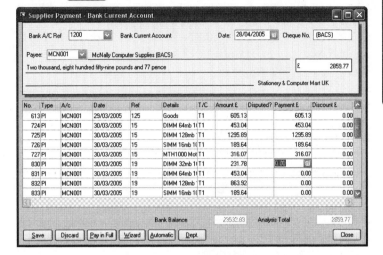

No.	Type	A/c	Date	Ref	Details	T/C	Amount £	Disputed?	Payment £	Discount £
613	PI	MCN001	29/03/2005	125	Goods	T1	605.13		605.13	0.00
724	PI	MCN001	30/03/2005	15	DIMM 64mb 1(	T1	453.04		453.04	0.00
725	PI	MCN001	30/03/2005	15	DIMM 128mb	T1	1295.89		1295.89	0.00
726	PI	MCN001	30/03/2005	15	SIMM 16mb 1(	T1	189.64		189.64	0.00
727	PI	MCN001	30/03/2005	15	MTH1000 Mot	T1	316.07		316.07	0.00
830	PI	MCN001	30/03/2005	19	DIMM 32mb 1(	T1	231.78		0.00	0.00
831	PI	MCN001	30/03/2005	19	DIMM 64mb 1(	T1	453.04		0.00	0.00
832	PI	MCN001	30/03/2005	19	DIMM 128mb	T1	863.92		0.00	0.00
833	PI	MCN001	30/03/2005	19	SIMM 16mb 1(	T1	189.64		0.00	0.00

Supplier Payment - Bank Current Account

Bank A/C Ref 1200   Bank Current Account   Date: 28/04/2005   Cheque No. (BACS)

Payee: MCN001   McNally Computer Supplies [BACS]

Two thousand, eight hundred fifty-nine pounds and 77 pence   £   2859.77

Stationery & Computer Mart UK

Bank Balance 23532.83   Analysis Total 2859.77

Save   Discard   Pay in Full   Wizard   Automatic   Dept.   Close

3 Set the **Date** and enter the **Cheque No.**, or leave this at (BACS).

4 Select the supplier from the **Payee** drop-down list.

Either

5 Enter the amount on the cheque and click [Automatic] to allocate this to invoices.

or

6 Select an invoice and enter an amount or click [Pay in Full].

or

7 If there is a discount, enter the full **Payment**, then the **Discount** – it will be deducted from the payment.

8 Click [Save]. In Accountant Plus and Financial Controller, if a cheque is required, the details will be added to the cheque list (see page 159).

9 Go back to step 3 for the next payment, or click [Close].

8.6 Batch payments

In the last chapter we met the Suggested Payments routine that could be run from the Supplier Credit Control window. Here is an alternative way to keep on top of your debts.

The Batch Purchase Payments window lists all the outstanding invoices – rather than the total owing to each supplier. While this does mean that you could be faced with a long list, it also enables you to pay invoices selectively if there have been any disputes over delivery, quality or prices.

The routine can only be started from the toolbar button, or from the context menu that appears when you right-click on the Bank Accounts window.

1 Select the Bank account from which payments are to be made.

Changing accounts

In all the other receipts and payments routines it is possible to select a different Bank account from within the routine. You cannot do this here, so do make sure you have the right account when you start.

---

2 Click [Batch] or select **Batch...** from the right-click menu.

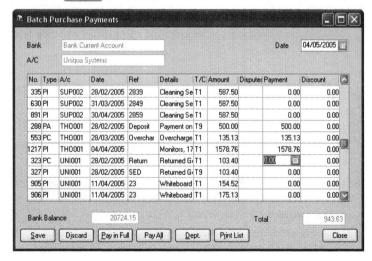

No.	Type	A/c	Date	Ref	Details	T/C	Amount	Disputed	Payment	Discount	
335	PI	SUP002	28/02/2005	2839	Cleaning Se	T1	587.50		0.00	0.00	
630	PI	SUP002	31/03/2005	2849	Cleaning Se	T1	587.50		0.00	0.00	
891	PI	SUP002	30/04/2005	2859	Cleaning Se	T1	587.50		0.00	0.00	
288	PA	THQ001	28/02/2005	Deposit	Payment on	T9	500.00		500.00	0.00	
553	PC	THQ001	28/03/2005	Overchar	Overcharge	T1	135.13		135.13	0.00	
1217	PI	THQ001	04/04/2005		Monitors, 17	T1	1578.76		1578.76	0.00	
323	PC	UNI001	28/02/2005	Return	Returned G	T1	103.40		0.00		0.00	
327	PI	UNI001	28/02/2005	SED	Returned G	T9	103.40		0.00	0.00	
905	PI	UNI001	11/04/2005	23	Whiteboard	T1	154.52		0.00	0.00	
906	PI	UNI001	11/04/2005	23	Whiteboard	T1	175.13		0.00	0.00	

Bank: Bank Current Account   Date: 04/05/2005
A/C: Unique Systems

Bank Balance: 20724.15   Total: 943.63

[Save] [Discard] [Pay in Full] [Pay All] [Dept.] [Print List] [Close]

3   If you want to pay all the invoices fully, click [Pay All]. (And if
    when you see the **Total** figure you decide that this is a mis-
    take, click [Discard] to clear all payments back to 0.00.)

4   Locate the invoices that you want to pay and either type in
    the amount or click [Pay in Full].

5   If there is a discount, enter the **Payment**, then the **Discount**.

6   Repeat 4 and 5 as required, then click [Save] and [Close].

8.7 Recurring entries

Direct debits, standing orders and other regular payments to
suppliers or from customers can be set up as recurring entries
and processed automatically.

There are two ways to view recurring entries and three ways to
start adding a new one. They all do the same job!

To add a recurring entry:

1   Click [Recurring] – this will open the **Recurring Entries** window.

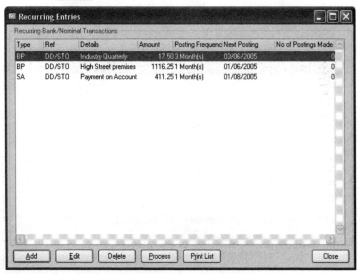

2 Click [Add] to open the **Add/Edit Recurring Entry** dialog box. (This can also be opened from the **New Recurring Transaction** task in the Bank window.)

You can make any type of payment into or out of the bank accounts

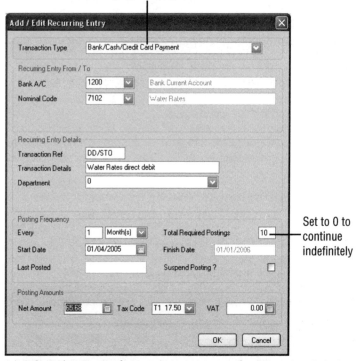

Set to 0 to continue indefinitely

3 Select the **Type** of transaction – it can be Payment, Receipt, Transfer (between bank accounts), on account payment from customer, or journal debit or credit.

Remember that every journal entry must have a matching debit or credit entry, and you must create these yourself.

4 Select the **Bank A/C** and **Nominal Code** that the payment is made from and to.

5 Enter the **Details** to identify the transaction.

6 Set the frequency, number of payments and date of the first one – leave the **Total Required Postings** at 0 if this payment is to be made regularly for the indefinite future.

7   Enter the **Net Amount**, and the tax if appropriate.

8   Click [OK] to return to the Recurring Entries window.

To view or post entries:

1   Click [Recurring].

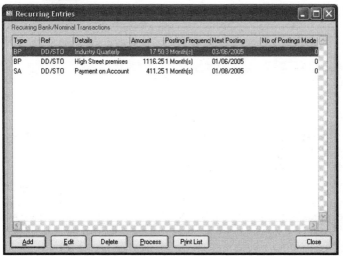

2   The **Recurring Entries** window lists the entries. If any need editing, now is your chance. Click [Edit] to do so.

3   If all is well, click [Process] to start posting the transactions.

4   At the **Process Recurring Entries** window, set the date up to which you want to show transactions.

5　If required, you can edit the **Due Date**, **Net** and **Tax** fields.

6　When you are happy that the entries are correct, click [Post].

◆　Now go and write the cheques. This routine does not do that for you – all it does is record the transactions.

To process recurring invoices:

Accountant Plus and Financial Controller only

1　Click the **Recurring List** in the Links in the **Bank** window.

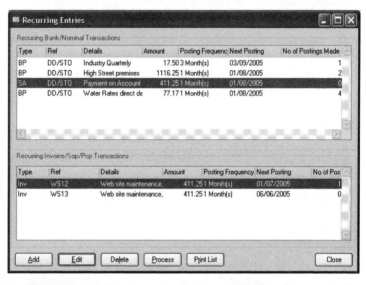

2　This **Recurring Entries** window lists the bank payments above and the invoices below. They are handled separately.

The payments pane acts like the standard Recurring Entries window. You can add, edit or delete entries from here.

The invoices pane is more limited. The Edit routine for these only allows you to change the frequency and dates – but no other invoice details.

3　Click [Process] to start. The same processing window will open as from the standard **Recurring Entries** window. After that has been dealt with, a second processing window will open to handle the invoices.

8.8 Cheque printing

Accountant Plus and Financial Controller have a neat facility to print the cheques that can arise from the payments routines.

- With **Make Payments,** in the Suppliers module, a cheque request is generated automatically, unless the supplier has been set for BACS payment.

- With **Payments** in the Bank module, a cheque request is generated if you click the Print Cheque button.

There are six ready-made layouts for printing cheques, with or without remittance slips, on pre-printed 12" or A4 paper. If none of these does the job, you can edit them or create your own print layouts in Report Designer.

1 In the Bank module, click ▣ Cheques or select Cheque List in the links.

Tick to see recently printed cheques

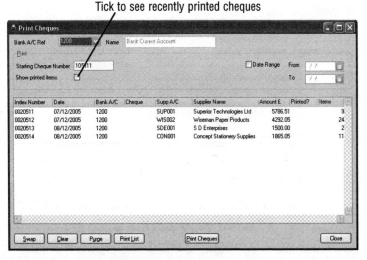

2 At the **Print Cheques** window, select the cheques you want to print – or select none to print them all.

3 Make sure that the **Starting Cheque Number** is correct.

4 Click Print Cheques.

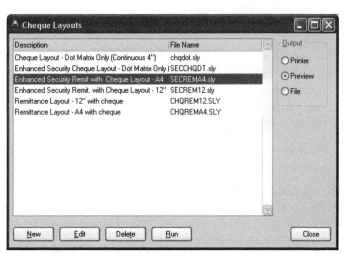

5   Select a layout and the output – and remember that if you pick **Preview**, you can carry on and print from there.

6   Click ⌈ Run ⌉.

7   The printout will be generated, and you will be asked if the cheques printed OK.

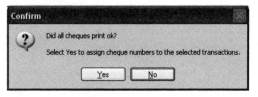

8   Click ⌈ Yes ⌉ to assign cheque numbers to the transactions and to mark them as printed in the cheque list.

Remittance advice slips

If payment is by BACS, or cheques are printed without remittance advice, or cheques are handwritten, you can print

remittance advice slips separately. Click 📋 Remittance in the Bank

module to open the Print Bank Remittances window. This lists all recent payments – select the ones for which you want advice slips.

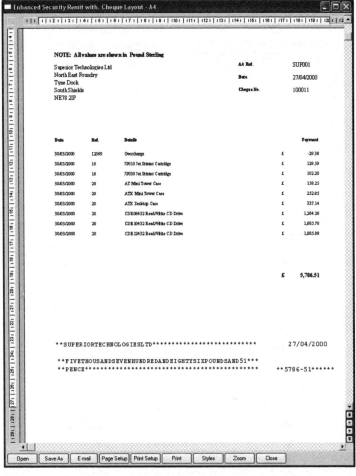

A cheque and remittance printout, designed for pre-printed stationery, seen in preview.

8.9 Transfers

The Transfer routine is used to record the movement of monies between Bank accounts, e.g. restocking petty cash, paying the credit card bill, or transferring cash between your current and deposit accounts at the bank.

1   Click 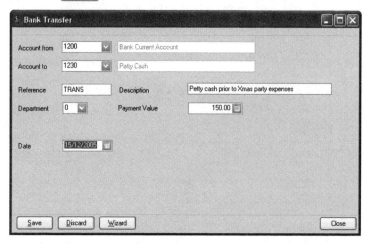 or select **Record Transfer** from the Tasks.

2   Select the **Account from** which to transfer.

3   Select the **Account to** which the money will be transferred.

4   Edit the **Description** if 'Bank Transfer' does not say enough for you.

5   Enter the **Payment Value**.

6   Set the **Date**.

7   Click [Save].

8   Repeat from step 2 if there are any more transfers, otherwise click [Close].

8.10 Statements

The Statement button can produce a list of the reconciled transactions, in numerical order and the running balance for all those accounts that have seen activity in the current audit trail. You can output statements for selected accounts only.

The process is kind of backwards – you tell it to run first, then define how to do it! Still, the result is the same.

1 Click 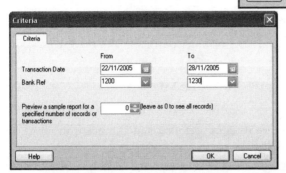 or select **Statement** in the Links area.

2 Select the **Output** mode and click `Run`.

3 At the **Criteria** dialog box, set the range by **Date** and/or **Bank Ref** if required, then click `OK`.

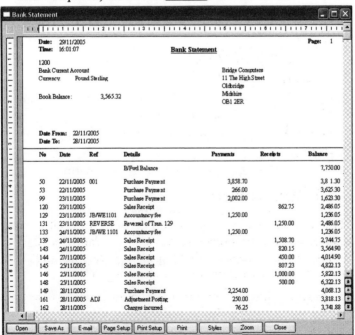

8.11 Reports

The Bank module offers over 40 summary and detailed reports, reflecting the accounts and transaction routines of the Bank module. The layouts are all fixed, but you control the content by setting the range of dates and reference numbers, and by selecting the Nominal and Bank accounts to include.

There are 14 sets of reports:

• Three varieties of **Bank payments and receipts**: together and separate, detailed and summary.

• **Cash payments** and **cash receipts**: detailed and summary.

• **Credit card payments** and **receipts**: detailed and summary.

• **Customer receipts**: detailed and summary, in all or just the cash sales.

• **Purchase and bank payments**: as a single report.

• **Reconciled transactions**: sorted in different ways.

• **Reconciled and unreconciled transactions**: and non-reconciled or purely unreconciled.

• **Sales and Bank receipts**: shown together.

• **Supplier payments**: detailed and summary.

And, of course, you can create your own reports, or edit any of these, using Report Designer (see Chapter 4).

Most reports can list all the accounts or those in a selected range. Depending upon the type of report, this can be based on the nominal code, date, transaction number or department.

1 Click ![Reports] or select **Reports** in the Links area.

2 Click ⊞ to open the folders and select a layout.

3 Choose the output from the drop-down list – Printer, Preview, File or E-mail.

4 Click [Generate Report].

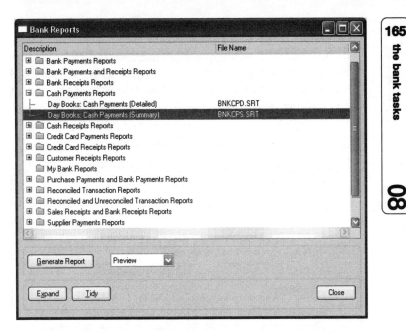

5 In the **Criteria** dialog box, you can specify a range of nominal codes, transaction dates or numbers.

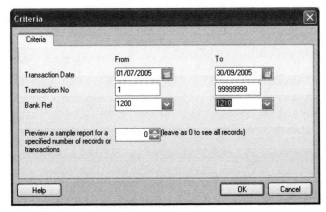

6 If you want to check that the criteria select the right things, set a number to preview, instead of running the full report.

7 Click [OK] to generate the report.

Summary

- Use the Bank module to view those Nominal accounts relating to bank, credit card and other money accounts, and to record the movement of money to, from and between them.

- The Bank accounts should be reconciled with the statements from the bank at regular intervals.

- Use the bank payments and receipts routines to record cash transactions.

- Use customer receipts to record money received from credit customers.

- Payments to your credit suppliers should be recorded through the supplier payments routine.

- Recurring payments can be set up and processed from this module.

- Accountant Plus and Financial Controller can print the cheques that can arise from the payments routines.

- The Statements routine produces lists of transactions through Bank accounts.

- Many different Reports are available in the Bank module.

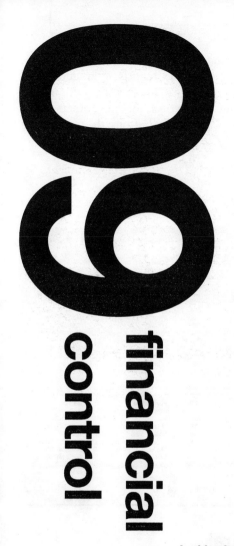

09

financial control

In this chapter you will learn:

- about the audit trail and how to clear it
- about the trial balance, profit and loss account and balance sheet
- about period end routines

9.1 Financials

The Financials display in the Company module gives one-stop access to the key financial tools and reports – the audit trail, month end and year end routines, trial balance, profit and loss account, balance sheet and VAT return, amongst others. Most of these can be accessed through toolbar buttons; the rest through the Tasks list.

1 Switch to the **Company** module.

2 Select **Financials** in the Links.

   You will see a list of all current transactions.

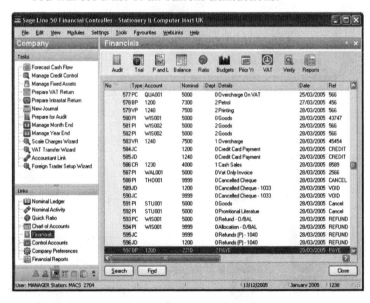

9.2 The Audit Trail

The Audit Trail is a key tool for monitoring and analysing your accounts. It is the record of those transactions that have not yet been fully processed, and those that have been processed but not yet cleared from the system.

The Audit Trail can be viewed, in summary form, in the Financials window. It can be printed out in the same form, or in briefer or more detailed forms through the **Audit** button. The printout routines also allow you to select the range of transactions by date, number, customer or supplier reference.

1 Click 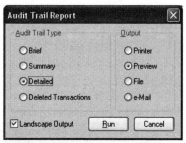.

2 Select the level of details.

3 Set the **Output** mode.

4 Click [Run].

Audit Trail Report

Audit Trail Type	Output
○ Brief	○ Printer
○ Summary	⊙ Preview
⊙ Detailed	○ File
○ Deleted Transactions	○ e-Mail

☑ Landscape Output   [Run]   [Cancel]

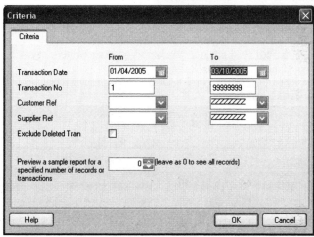

Criteria

Criteria

	From	To
Transaction Date	01/04/2005	03/10/2005
Transaction No	1	99999999
Customer Ref		////////
Supplier Ref		////////
Exclude Deleted Tran	☐	

Preview a sample report for a specified number of records or transactions   0 (leave as 0 to see all records)

[Help]   [OK]   [Cancel]

5 At the **Criteria** dialog, define the range to display, or leave the settings at the defaults to show all current transactions.

6 Click [OK].

Mark a clear trail!

Make sure that you have a full printout of the audit trail before running the clear routine (page 180).

Part of a detailed audit printout. The landscape mode works better as there is so much information in each line.

The Type codes

These codes are used in the Type column:

BP	Bank Payment	BR	Bank Receipt
JC	Journal Credit	JD	Journal Debit
PC	Purchase Credit	PI	Purchase Invoice
PP	Purchase Payment	SA	Sale, payment on account
SC	Sale, Credit	SI	Sale, Invoice
SR	Sale Receipt		

9.3 The Trial Balance

In a manual system, the main purpose of the Trial Balance is to check that every credit has its matching debit, and vice versa. This is less of an issue in Line 50 where most of the double-entries are handled for you. However, there are opportunities for human error, and the Trial Balance will tell you if further investigation is needed. It also provides a convenient summary of the nominal ledger accounts.

The Trial Balance is based on the data from the start of the year up to a chosen month – and, apart from the output mode, that is your only option.

1 Click 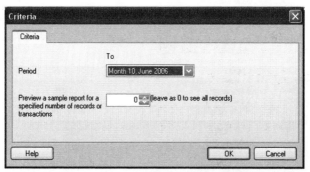.

2 Set the **Output** mode and click ☐ Run ☐.

3 At the **Criteria** dialog box, select the end month. If you just want a small sample to check the output style, enter the number of accounts you want to see. Click ☐ OK ☐.

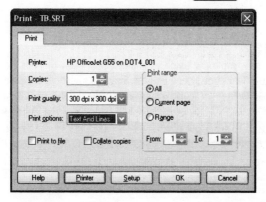

4 If you are outputting to the printer, set the options. Note the Print options list – you can print text with or without lines, and there's a Quick Text setting. Click ☐ OK ☐.

```
Date:      18/10/2005              Bridge Computers                    Page:  1
Time:      19:11:16               Period Trial Balance

To Period:     Month 10, June 2006

N/C        Name                                        Debit          Credit
0020       Plant and Machinery                      18,000.00
0030       Office Equipment                          5,400.00
0040       Furniture and Fixtures                    1,240.00
0050       Van                                      11,410.00
1001       Stock                                    11,800.00
1100       Debtors Control Account                   1,562.38
1200       Bank Current Account                                      1,275.32
1210       Bank Deposit Account                      1,054.26
1220       Building Society Account                    500.00
1230       Petty Cash                                  145.74
1240       Company Credit Card                                       1,022.05
1250       Credit Card Receipts                        125.60
2100       Creditors Control Account                                 4,702.66
2200       Sales Tax Control Account                                   442.74
2201       Purchase Tax Control Account                939.86
2202       VAT Liability                                               328.00
3001       Owners Investment                                        20,000.00
4000       Computer systems                                         46,637.00
4001       Peripherals and parts                                    56,960.00
4002       Software package                                         49,197.00
4100       Consultancy                                 250.00
5000       Materials Purchased                      63,033.96
6201       Advertising                               1,500.00
7001       Directors Salaries                       24,000.00
7004       Wages - Regular                          29,950.00
7100       Rent                                      4,005.00
7102       Water Rates                                 262.72
7103       General Rates                             1,010.00
7200       Electricity                               2,000.00
7502       Telephone                                 1,500.00
7601       Audit and Accountancy Fees                1,250.00
7900       Bank Interest Paid                           76.25
8201       Subscriptions                                17.50
9998       Suspense Account                                            468.50
                                        Totals:    181,033.27       181,033.27
```

A Trial Balance, produced using simple test data – any real one would have a lot more to it than this. Notice that the Suspense Account shows a balance: £468.50 has been mis-recorded somewhere along the line. This needs investigating. Open the Suspense Account and look at the Details tab, to see the months in which the balance appeared. Then switch to the Activity tab to locate the unbalanced transactions in that month.

Output for export?

Output to File is worth considering on any of these financial reports. If the data is saved as either text or CSV (Comma Separated Values), it can be imported into a spreadsheet for further analysis.

9.4 The Profit and Loss account

With the Profit and Loss account, you define the period, allowing you to examine a month or quarter at any point of the year. You can also select the chart of accounts, if you have set up one or more of your own (see page 77 for more on creating charts of accounts).

1 Click [P and L] in the toolbar of the **Financials** window.

2 Set the **Output** mode and click [Run].

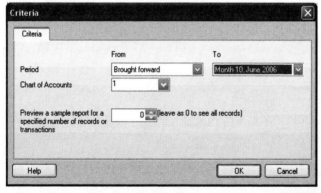

3 At the **Criteria** dialog box, select the months to include **From** and **To**.

4 If there are several charts of accounts, select the one to use.

5 Click [OK].

6 If you are outputting to file, the **Save As** dialog box will open. Set the **Save in** folder and **Filename** as usual, then drop-down the **Save as type** list and select one of the CSV settings.

Save As

Save in: 🗁 REPORTS

📁 Assets	📁 Invoice	📁 Supplier
📁 Audit	📁 Nominal	
📁 Bank	📁 POP	
📁 Customer	📁 Products	
📁 Excel	📁 Project	
📁 Finance	📁 SOP	

File name: pandjune05   [Save]

Save as type: Report Data Files (*.srd)   [Cancel]

> Report Data Files (*.srd)
> Comma Separated Files (*.csv)
> Delimited Files (*.csv)
> Text Files (*.txt)
> HTML Files (Browser) (*.htm)
> HTML Files (Word) (*.html)
> PDF file (*.pdf)

7 Click [Save].

Date:	19/10/2005	**Bridge Computers**		Page:	1
Time:	10:17:09	Profit & Loss			

From: Brought forward
To: Month 10, June 2006
Chart of Accounts: Default Layout of Accounts

		Period		Year to Date	
Sales					
Product Sales		152,794.00		152,794.00	
Services		(250.00)		(250.00)	
			152,544.00		152,544.00
Purchases					
Purchases		63,033.96		63,033.96	
			63,033.96		63,033.96
Direct Expenses					
Sales Promotion		1,500.00		1,500.00	
			1,500.00		1,500.00
	Gross Profit/(Loss):		88,010.04		88,010.04
Overheads					
Gross Wages		53,950.00		53,950.00	
Rent and Rates		5,277.72		3,115.00	
Heat, Light and Power		2,000.00		2,000.00	
Printing and Stationery		1,500.00		1,500.00	
Professional Fees		1,250.00		1,250.00	
Bank Charges and Interest		76.25		76.25	
General Expenses		17.50		0.00	
Suspense & Mispostings		(468.50)		0.00	
			63,602.97		61,891.25
	Net Profit/(Loss):		24,407.07		26,118.79

A sample Profit and Loss display, based on the same figures as the earlier
Trial Balance.

9.5 The Balance Sheet

The Balance Sheet – and the Budget and Prior Year outputs – have the same options as the Profit and Loss account. As with that, output to file for further analysis, is a common choice.

1 Click [Budgets].

2 Set the **Output** mode and click [Run].

3 At the **Criteria** dialog box, select the months to include **From** and **To**.

4 If there are several charts of accounts, select the one to use.

5 Click [OK].

6 If you are outputting to file, set the options and click [Save].

Date: 19/12/2005	**Bridge Computers**	**Page:** 1
Time: 10:35:11	**Balance Sheet**	

From: Brought forward
To: Month 10, June 2006

Chart of Account: Default Layout of Accounts

	Period		Year to Date	
Fixed Assets				
Plant and Machinery	18,000.00		18,000.00	
Office Equipment	5,400.00		5,400.00	
Furniture and Fixtures	1,240.00		1,240.00	
Motor Vehicles	11,410.00		11,410.00	
		36,050.00		36,050.00
Current Assets				
Stock	11,800.00		11,800.00	
Debtors	1,562.38		1,562.38	
Deposits and Cash	1,700.00		1,700.00	
Credit Card (Debtors)	125.60		125.60	
VAT Liability	169.12		169.12	
		15,357.10		15,357.10
Current Liabilities				
Creditors : Short Term	4,702.66		4,702.66	
Credit Card (Creditors)	1,022.05		1,022.05	
Bank Account	1,275.32		1,275.32	
		7,000.03		7,000.03
Current Assets less Current Liabilities:		8,357.07		8,357.07
Total Assets less Current Liabilities:		44,407.07		44,407.07
Long Term Liabilities				
		0.00		0.00
Total Assets less Total Liabilities:		44,407.07		44,407.07
Capital & Reserves				
Share Capital	20,000.00		20,000.00	
P&L Account	24,407.07		26,118.79	
Previous Year Adj			(1,711.72)	
		44,407.07		44,407.07

A Balance Sheet seen in Preview mode.

9.6 Verification

The verification routines can be used to check your data before you run the VAT Return. There are four possible routines.

1 Click 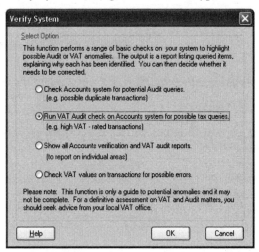.

2 At the **Verify System** dialog box select the type of verification.

Verify System

Select Option

This function performs a range of basic checks on your system to highlight possible Audit or VAT anomalies. The output is a report listing queried items, explaining why each has been identified. You can then decide whether it needs to be corrected.

○ Check Accounts system for potential Audit queries.
   (e.g. possible duplicate transactions)

⊙ Run VAT Audit check on Accounts system for possible tax queries.
   (e.g. high VAT - rated transactions)

○ Show all Accounts verification and VAT audit reports.
   (to report on individual areas)

○ Check VAT values on transactions for possible errors.

Please note: This function is only a guide to potential anomalies and it may not be complete. For a definitive assessment on VAT and Audit matters, you should seek advice from your local VAT office.

| Help | | OK | Cancel |

3 You may need to define this more closely – if you have a lot of transactions, it may be better to look at only one thing at a time.

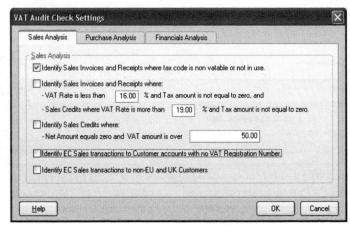

VAT Audit Check Settings

| Sales Analysis | Purchase Analysis | Financials Analysis |

Sales Analysis

☑ Identify Sales Invoices and Receipts where tax code is non vatable or not in use.

☐ Identify Sales Invoices and Receipts where:

- VAT Rate is less than [16.00] % and Tax amount is not equal to zero, and

- Sales Credits where VAT Rate is more than [19.00] % and Tax amount is not equal to zero.

☐ Identify Sales Credits where:

- Net Amount equals zero and VAT amount is over [50.00]

☐ Identify EC Sales transactions to Customer accounts with no VAT Registration Number.

☐ Identify EC Sales transactions to non-EU and UK Customers

| Help | | OK | Cancel |

financial control

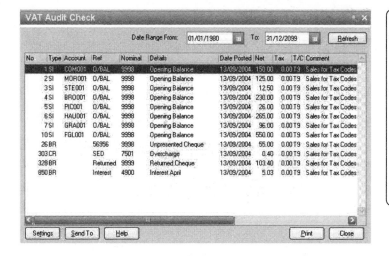

9.7 VAT

I like the way VAT is handled – for two reasons. First, Line 50 does all the work for you! And second, the window follows the design of the standard VAT form, just as that the payments screen mimics a cheque, and that makes transferring figures a breeze.

1 Click to open the VAT Return window.

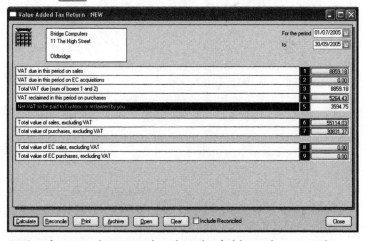

2 Set the period start and end in the fields at the top right.

3 If you want to **Include Reconciled** transactions, tick the box.

4 Click [Calculate]. If there are also unreconciled transactions, you will be told and can choose whether to include them.

5 If you want a report, click [Print].

6 Select the **VAT Return Type** and the **Output** mode.

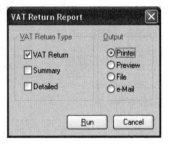

The **Summary** report shows the total VAT due on each account; **Detailed** shows every transaction that had a VAT component.

7 Click [Run].

8 Calculating VAT has no effect on your data, so you can do it as often as need be – e.g. you may want to run it early to get an idea of the likely amount to pay. Once you have done the final calculation for a period, click [Reconcile] to mark the items as processed so that they do not appear in future returns.

9 Click [Close] when you have done.

9.8 Managing the month end

The month end routines are optional. Their purpose is to handle recurring entries, update stock and asset valuations and tidy up the customer and supplier accounts, so that you don't have to wade through old data, but to do this without losing essential information. They take time to run, but could save time overall. Look closely at your accounts and talk to your accountant.

There are quite a few steps involved in performing the month end routines, but fortunately Line 50 gives you a checklist of things to do, and direct links to each operation.

1 In the **Company** module, select **Manage Month End** in the **Tasks** pane. The **Period End** Help display will appear. In the first stage you will be guided through the operations to tidy up the accounts for the month: posting current transactions,

There are Help pages to guide you through the month end procedures – this is the first stage.

Direct link to the operation

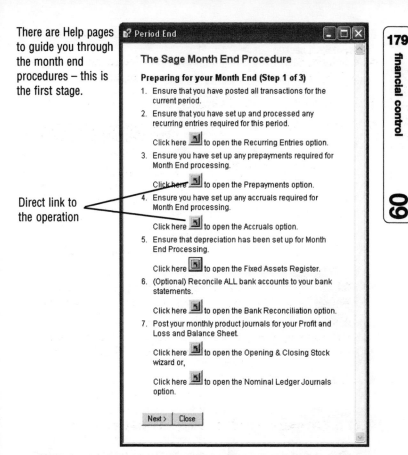

Period End

The Sage Month End Procedure

Preparing for your Month End (Step 1 of 3)

1. Ensure that you have posted all transactions for the current period.

2. Ensure that you have set up and processed any recurring entries required for this period.

   Click here to open the Recurring Entries option.

3. Ensure you have set up any prepayments required for Month End processing.

   Click here to open the Prepayments option.

4. Ensure you have set up any accruals required for Month End processing.

   Click here to open the Accruals option.

5. Ensure that depreciation has been set up for Month End Processing.

   Click here to open the Fixed Assets Register.

6. (Optional) Reconcile ALL bank accounts to your bank statements.

   Click here to open the Bank Reconciliation option.

7. Post your monthly product journals for your Profit and Loss and Balance Sheet.

   Click here to open the Opening & Closing Stock wizard or,

   Click here to open the Nominal Ledger Journals option.

Next >   Close

dealing with recurring entries, prepayments and accruals, recording depreciation and updating the stock. Some of these may not be relevant to your business or the way you handle your accounts (e.g. do you need to revalue your fixed assets monthly?), and some are not present in the Accountant version of the software.

2   At the second stage, you will be prompted to make a backup so have your backup media ready. After setting the program date to the month end date, the month end procedure is run.

3   The **Month End...** dialog box has four options – check those which are relevant and click [OK].

Your data is vital –
always take a backup
before making any
changes to your files

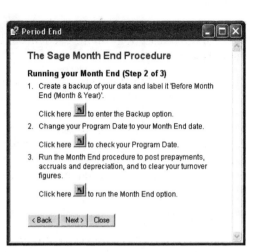

The Month End procedure is activated
during the second stage

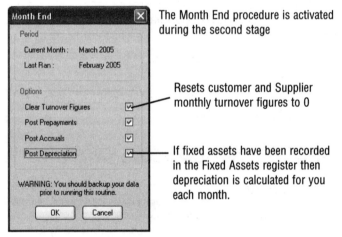

Resets customer and Supplier
monthly turnover figures to 0

If fixed assets have been recorded
in the Fixed Assets register then
depreciation is calculated for you
each month.

4 At the third stage you will be prompted to create a second
backup. The remaining steps are optional. You can clear your
stock activity and/or the audit trail. And if you do either or
both of these, you will need to take another backup after-
wards. Let's have a closer look at clearing the audit trail.

Clearing the Audit Trail

Clearing removes all those transactions that have been fully paid,
reconciled with the bank statement and processed for the VAT

return. And before they are erased, the routine calculates the effect of the transactions on the accounts and rewrites the opening balances.

How long you keep transactions in the Audit Trail is for you and your accountant to decide. The Line 50 system is capable of storing up to 2 billion transactions so space is not an issue (as long as your hard disk is big enough and your backup media can cope with the file sizes). Speed – or rather the lack of it – may become an issue, as response time can slow down with very large files. Normal practice is for the Audit Trail to be cleared as part of your regular end of period routines.

To clear the audit trail:

1 You must have hard copies of all your transactions before you clear the trail. Print the reports for the Audit Trail, Monthly Day Books, Sales, Purchase and Nominal Activity and VAT Return.

2 If you have not done so already, backup your data.

3 Start the Clear Audit Trail wizard from stage 3 of the Month End routine, or open the **Tools** menu, point to **Period End** and select **Clear Audit Trail**.

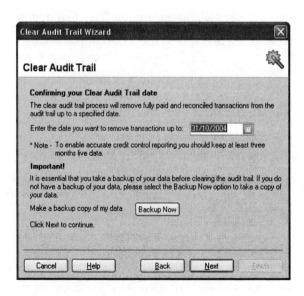

4 Read the prompts and warnings as you work through the wizard. At the third stage, enter the date to clear up to – this will typically be the last month end.

5 When the wizard has done its work, you will be offered a chance to view the transactions that have been cleared. View them, and print the report for your records. You cannot be too careful with your data.

9.9 The Year End routine

The Year End procedure is a little simpler than that of the Month End – its main purpose is to transfer summary figures to the Prior Year – and it must be preceded by the Month End routine for month 12, where the bulk of the work is done.

Backups and printouts to secure old data are key parts of this procedure, so have your backup media and paper ready!

1 Select **Manage Year End** in the Tasks. The **Period End** Help display will appear. Work through it, clicking 🔳 as needed to go back into the system to run backups, printing and other operations.

2 In Step 2 of the Help pages, run the Year End option.

3 At the **Year End** dialog box, select the **Output** mode – *Printer* or *File*.

4 If you use the budgeting facilities, tick the checkboxes to transfer the actual figures to the budgets, and to generate next year's budgets (setting increases if appropriate).

5 Double check that you have all the necessary backups and printouts, and if you have, click [OK] to run the routine.

6 The final stages of the Year End procedure are about tidying up – clearing old data and removing accounts which are no longer in use.

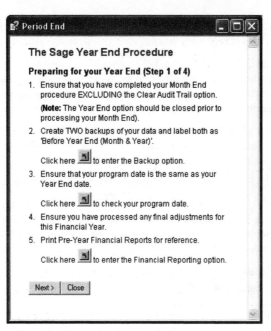

The Period End Help window for the Year End procedures.

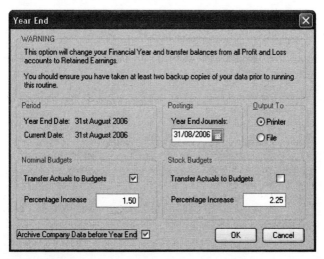

The Year End dialog box.

Summary

♦ The Audit Trail is the full record of all transactions that are still awaiting further processing. It should be cleared as part of the end of period routines to remove fully reconciled transactions.

♦ The Trial Balance provides a summary of the state of the accounts – and if it doesn't balance, worry! If there are values in Suspense or Mispostings, investigate!

♦ The Profit and Loss account and Balance Sheet are based on a selected Chart of Accounts.

♦ Line 50 will calculate the figures for the VAT return and display them in the same layout as the VAT form. Before running the VAT routine you should verify your data.

♦ The end of month and end of year routines tidy up the system and calculate new end of period totals.

10

products

In this chapter you will learn:

- how to create product records
- how to view and edit product records
- about price lists and pricing structures
- how to record stock movements

10.1 The Products module

The Products module is one of the less interactive parts of the system – which figures, as there is not a lot you can do with the products, except keep a track of them and use product information in the creation of invoices. The tools in this window let you create new product records, edit existing records, update stock levels, maintain price lists and print the information.

If you have a large inventory, maintaining full, accurate product and price lists can be quite time-consuming, but it delivers faster, more efficient invoicing and should save much more time in the long run.

Product Record Wizard   Stock movements

Product Defaults

Before you do any work on your products, check and set the defaults – see page 66.

10.2 New Products

New product records are set up through a wizard. This will ask for a wide range of details, not all of which may be relevant to your business. Don't waste time entering useless information. If any details are not known when you are working on the wizard, leave them and enter them later by editing the product record.

* The **Description, Code, Sale Price, Tax Code, Unit of Sale** and **Nominal Code** are essential.

* **Location, Commodity Code, Weight, Purchase A/C** code and (supplier's) **Part No.** can be often omitted.

1 In the **Product** window, click .

2 Click **Next** to get past the first page and enter a **Description**. The **Code** will be created from this – edit it if necessary.

3 Enter the **Location, Category** and other details if wanted.

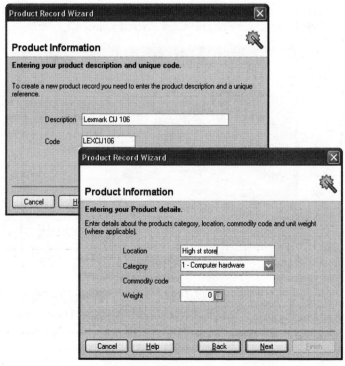

4 Enter the **Sale Price,** and change the **Sales Nominal Code, Unit of Sale, Tax Code** and **Department** if the defaults do not suit.

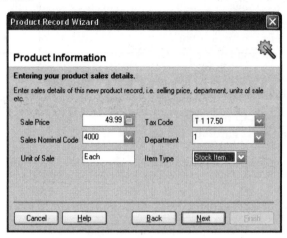

5 Select the **Supplier A/C** and enter the **Part No., Re-Order Level** and **Quantity** and **Cost Price** if wanted.

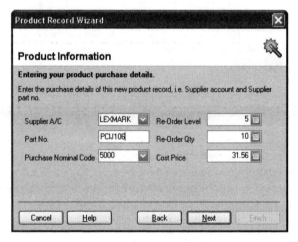

6 You will be asked if you want to set an opening balance. If you do, select **Yes** then enter the **Reference, Date, Quantity** and **Cost Price** – this is the price per unit, not the total.

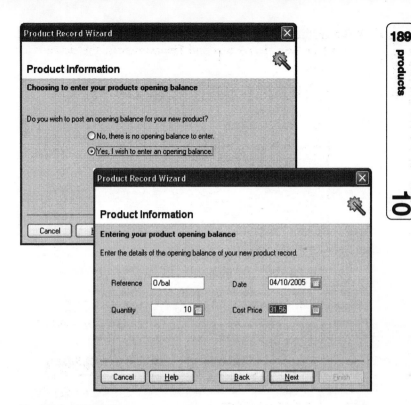

7 Click [Finish].

10.3 Viewing and editing product data

The product records contain the information that you entered
when you first created it, plus details of any sales or other stock
movements. There is also a Memo tab for any notes you want to
add, a BOM (bill of materials) tab, where the components of a
compound product can be listed, and a Web tab which can hold
images and text for use in web pages.

If prices or other details have changed, or if there are errors or
omissions in your product data, the records are easily edited.

1 Select the record(s) you want to edit.

2 Click [Record].

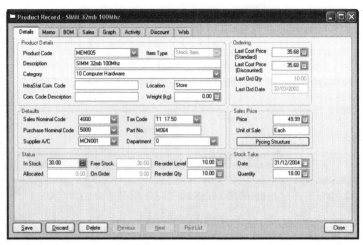

3 Edit the record. Add details to the **Memo** tab if required.

4 If the product is made up from separate components – each with their own product record – switch to the **BOM** tab. Select each component in the **Product Code** field, and set the **Quantity** value – Line 50 will fill the remaining fields.

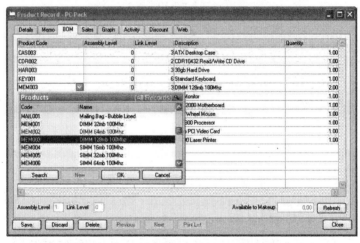

5 Click [Save].

6 Click [Next] if there are more records, or select a new record from the **Product Code** at the top left and repeat steps 3 to 5.

7 Click [Close].

> ## Creating Product records while invoicing
>
> If, while generating an invoice, you find that a product is not on the system, click the New button on the Products list. A product record window will open to collect essential details.

10.4 Price lists

If you sell products at different prices according to the nature of the customer – as opposed to, or as well as, giving discounts to categories of customers – these can be handled by Line 50.

A price list has two aspects: the products and their prices, and the customers to whom those prices apply. If price lists exist, when you add a product to an invoice, Line 50 will check the lists to see which price to use for the customer. If the customer is not on any list, the standard price will be applied.

To create a price list:

1 Click ![Prices] or select **Price Lists** in the Links.

2 At the **Price Lists** window, click [New].

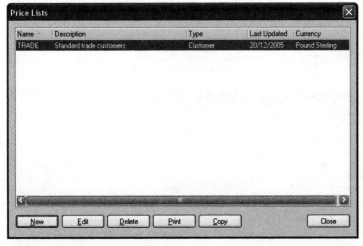

3 You will be asked which type of price list you wish to create. Click [Customer]. (Supplier lists are a bit different, but simpler.)

4 At the **New Price List** window, enter a **Name** and a **Description** for the list. Click [Add] to add the first product to the list. (The window will change its title to **Edit Price List**.)

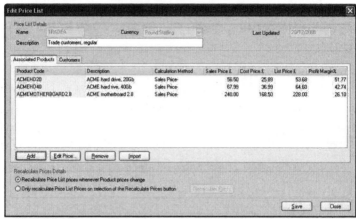

5 At the **Add Products** dialog box, select an item from the list.

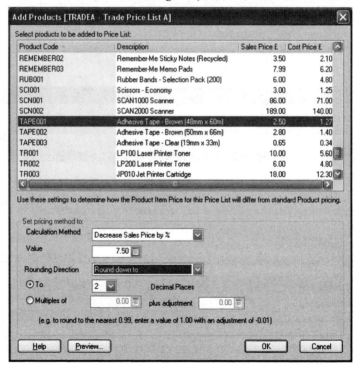

6 You can set a fixed price, or decrease or increase the standard price by a percentage or a value. As percentage changes can produce fractional amounts, these can be rounded up or down. You can also work in multiples with an adjustment, e.g. whole pounds minus 1p to give 3.99, 6.99 prices.

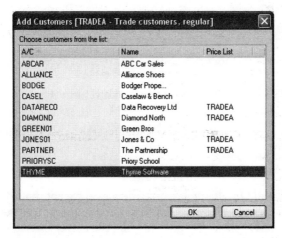

7 Click ⌞ OK ⌟ to add the product and its price to the list.

8 Click ⌞ Add ⌟ and repeat steps 5 to 7 for the other products.

9 Switch to the **Customers** tab.

10 Click ⌞ Add ⌟.

11 Select a customer to whom the price will apply. Click ⌞ OK ⌟.

12 Repeat 10 and 11 to add all the relevant customers to the list, then click ⌞ Save ⌟ and ⌞ Close ⌟.

10.5 Stock levels

The Product records can be used to keep track of stock levels. You can enter the quantities in stock when first setting up a record or after a stocktake. If goods are sold via invoices, the movements out are automatically marked on the product record when the invoice is posted. Deliveries, non-invoiced sales and other movements are handled through the In and Out routines in the Product module.

Stock movements

The Products module has three routines for recording changes:

 Adjustment in – deliveries and returns.

 Adjustment out – sales and losses.

 Updating the files after a manual stocktake.

The In and Out dialog boxes are identical except that the In box also has a field to record the current cost, and in the Out dialog box this is replaced by one showing the current stock levels.

To record movement:

1 Select the products to be adjusted. This is not essential as products can be selected at step 3, but it may be simpler to select them all at the start.

2 Click [In] or [Out].

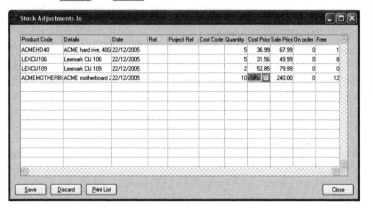

Product Code	Details	Date	Ref.	Project Ref	Cost Code	Quantity	Cost Price	Sale Price	On order	Free
ACMEHD40	ACME hard rive, 40G	22/12/2005				5	36.99	67.99	0	1
LEXCIJ106	Lexmark CIJ 106	22/12/2005				5	31.56	49.99	0	8
LEXCIJ109	Lexmark CIJ 109	22/12/2005				2	52.85	79.99	0	0
ACMEMOTHERB(	ACME motherboard 2	22/12/2005				10	67.25	240.00	0	12

[Save] [Discard] [Print List]   [Close]

3 Select the **Product Code**, if necessary.

4 The **Date** will be set to the program date. Adjust if necessary.

5 Enter a **Ref** and/or **Project Ref** if required.

6 Enter the **Quantity**.

7 With In movements, change the **Cost Price** if it is different from the default.

8 Repeat steps 3 to 7 for other products.

9 Click [Save].

10 Click [Close].

To run a stocktake:

1 Select the products, or leave this until step 3.

2 Click [Stk Take].

3 Select the **Product Code**, if necessary.

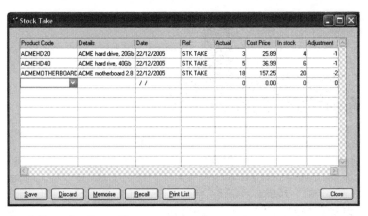

4 Adjust the **Date** if necessary.

5 Enter the **Actual** number in stock.

6 Repeat steps 3 to 5 for other products.

7 Click [Save] then [Close].

Summary

+ Product records are produced through the Product Record Wizard. Non-essential information can be omitted or added later.

+ In the Products module you can create new product records, edit old records, update stock levels and print details of your products.

+ Details can be edited at any time, simply select the records and click the Record button to start.

+ Price lists allow you to maintain different pricing structures for different categories of customer.

+ Stock levels are updated as goods are sold through invoices, and can also be adjusted through the In, Out and Stock Take routines.

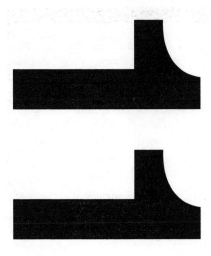

11

help and support

In this chapter you will learn:

- about browsing the Help system
- how to locate Help through the index or a search
- about advice and support from Sage on the Web
- about the shortcut keys

11.1 Help

Sage Line 50 systems have very many features. Some of these you may never use, as they are not applicable to your business, others will be used only rarely, at year-ends or when particular problems arise. So, though you will soon be at ease with the routine chores – most of which should be covered in this book – there will be times when you find yourself saying, 'How do I do this?' At times like this, turn first to the Help pages. To find information, you can browse through the **Contents**, look it up in the **Index** or **Search** for it.

If the Help pages alone do not provide the answer, there is more information, technical support and other types of Help available online at Sage's website.

11.2 Contents

The Contents panel offers the best approach when you are looking for Help with a module or operation. Here, the Help pages are organized into sections, with two or three levels of subdivisions. If the first page that you find does not tell you quite what you want to know, look for the links to related pages, and follow these up to find the answer.

◆ Look in the *Welcome* and *Setting up* sections for Help with the use of the software.

◆ Look in the *Accounts and Bookkeeping Information* section for Help with accounting concepts and techniques.

◆ Look in the *Glossary* for explanations of accounting or computing terms.

1 Open the **Help** menu and click **Contents and Index**.

2 If necessary, click the **Contents** tab.

3 Click ❦ to open a section. Most have subsections – click ❦ again to reach the pages.

4 Click ? to display a page in the main pane.

5 Click on words with a <u>solid underline</u> to find out more.

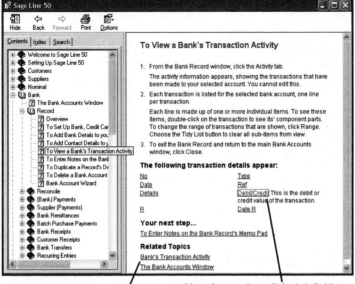

List of terms have linked definitions

Many pages have links to related topics

With single words in simple lists, clicking will usually display an explanation of the term – click again to hide it.

With other linked text – especially under **Related Topics** and **Your next step…** headings – a click takes you to linked pages.

6 Once you have viewed more than one page, the **Back** button becomes active – click it to work back though those earlier Help pages.

7 The **Help** window sits on top of the other Line 50 windows. When you have done, click ☒ to close it or ▪ to minimize it out of the way if you want to refer to it again later.

11.3 The Help Index

The Index contains well over 2000 entries and sub-entries, in alphabetical order. You can scroll through to find an entry, but it is quicker to type in the first few letters of a word and jump to the relevant part of the Index.

Most entries lead to a single page, but sometimes you will be offered a choice of pages from the same word.

If you were using the Index when you last shut down Help, the **Contents and Index** option will reopen Help at the Index.

1 Open the **Help** menu and select **Contents and Index**.

2 If necessary, click the **Index** tab.

3 Drag the slider to scroll through the index.

or

4 Type the first few letters of the word to jump to the right part of the list.

5 Select an entry and click Display .

6 If the **Topics Found** panel opens to offer you a choice – select one and click Display .

11.4 Searching for Help

A Search hunts through the entire text of the Help system. It normally produces more results, as it will find every page containing a given word – not just the main ones on the topic. This can be useful as you can get a more thorough understanding of an issue by following up all the leads, but if all you want to do is find the meaning of a word, or learn how to do a particular job, it can take a bit longer to locate the relevant page.

If you were using the Search when you last shut down Help, the **Contents and Index** option reopens Help at the **Search** panel.

1 Open the **Help** menu or click the **Help** button and select **Contents and Index**.

2 If necessary, click the **Search** tab.

3 Type one or more words to define the Help you need.

4 Click ![List Topics]

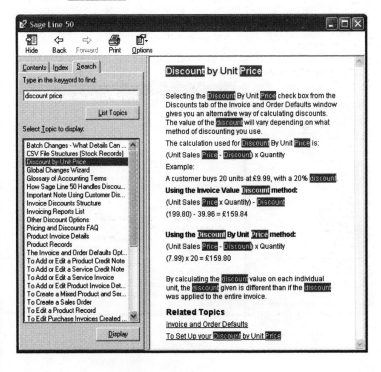

5   Select a topic from the bottom pane.

6   Click   Display .

11.5 The navigation panel

If you want to work on your accounts while keeping the Help window open, you may need to adjust your screen display so that you can see what you are doing.

Like any other window, the Help window can be resized and moved, but the most effective way to reduce its size is to hide the navigation panel. You can still go back through recently opened pages, or follow links from the current page, and if you need to get back into it, to find a different Help page, it is easily opened again.

1   Click [Hide icon] to close the navigation panel.

2   Work through your task, using the Help page for guidance as needed.

3   Click [Show icon] if you need to open the navigation panel again.

You can still print and move back and forwards in the reduced window.

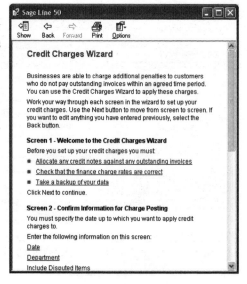

Credit Charges Wizard

Businesses are able to charge additional penalties to customers who do not pay outstanding invoices within an agreed time period. You can use the Credit Charges Wizard to apply these charges.

Work your way through each screen in the wizard to set up your credit charges. Use the Next button to move from screen to screen. If you want to edit anything you have entered previously, select the Back button.

Screen 1 - Welcome to the Credit Charges Wizard

Before you set up your credit charges you must:
* Allocate any credit notes against any outstanding invoices
* Check that the finance charge rates are correct
* Take a backup of your data

Click Next to continue.

Screen 2 - Confirm Information for Charge Posting

You must specify the date up to which you want to apply credit charges to.

Enter the following information on this screen:

Date

Department

Include Disputed Items

11.6 Sage on the Web

The options on the WebLinks menu connect you to the Internet and take you to Sage's website. The public part of the site contains mainly news and information about Sage's products and services, though it also has some good articles on major topics.

SageCover subscribers have access to a section where they can get advice and assistance with Sage systems and with accountancy and other aspects of business in general.

1 Open the **Weblinks** menu and select **SageCover Home**.

2 The big tabs on the left switch between the main areas of the site – most of us will want to be in the Customers area. Click to go there.

3 Use the links listed on the left to go to the various advice and support sections, or those across the top to go to other parts of the site.

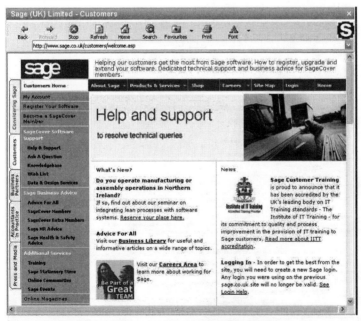

Notice that there are several categories of advice and some are only open to Sage Cover members. The Knowledgebase is also for members only.

SageCover

SageCover is available free for the first six weeks after purchasing Sage software. Continuing cover can be bought online from the Sage shop. The cost varies depending upon the software, the number of users and the level of support required.

11.7 The Knowledgebase

One of the benefits of SageCover is access to the Knowledgebase. This has articles across a wide range of business and accounting activities. You can browse through them, to see what is available on any given topic, or use the Ask a Question approach to get specific Help from the database. This is usually the quickest way to locate the information that you need – just enter one or more keywords to focus the search.

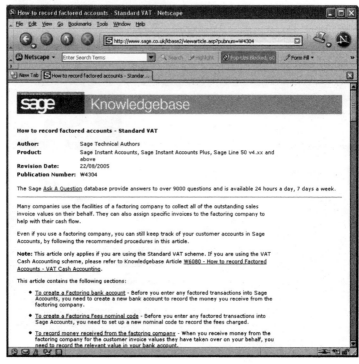

- If you can't find an answer in the Knowledgebase, go to **Ask Support** and e-mail your problem to their support staff.

1 Go to **SageCover Home** and switch to the **Customers** area.

2 Click the **Knowledgebase** link.

3 Select your accounts system.

4 If you have not already logged in, you need to do so now before you can get any further.

5 Select a topic heading to browse through the articles.

or

6 Click the **Ask a Question** link.

7 Type in one or more keywords and start the search.

8 You will see a list of matching articles, click one to read.

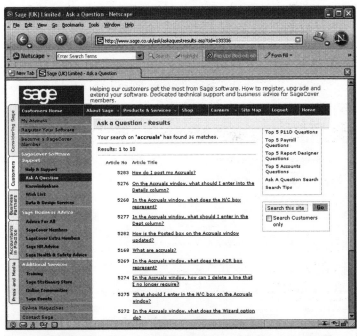

There are over 9000 articles in the Knowledgebase! Asking very specific questions can help to locate the right information, but sometimes it is better to use only a single keyword and then browse the results.

11.8 Shortcut keys

When the Sage system is active, the function keys [F1] to [F12] all have special purposes.

Check these out after you have been using the Sage system for a little while and see which ones it would be useful to learn. Though all functions can be accessed easily through the menus or toolbar buttons, when you are typing it is handy to be able to get to them directly from the keyboard.

You might like to note these in particular:

[F1]   Displays the Help system.

[F2]   Runs Windows calculator – the results of the calculations can be copied and pasted back into a Line 50 field.

[F3]   Opens the Edit Line window when creating an invoice (or while processing orders in Financial Controller).

[F4]   Displays the drop-down list, calendar or calculator from the current field when invoicing, etc.

[F5]   Displays the currency convertor when used from a numeric field or the spell checker from a text field.

[F7]   Inserts a line into an invoice.

[F8]   Deletes the current line of an invoice.

[F9]   Calculates the VAT from a net price.

[F12] Launches Report Designer.

Summary

- There is plenty of Help available. You can browse through the Contents, or search for information in the Index or Search panels.

- If you want to refer to the Help window while working in the Sage window, you can hide its navigation panel so it takes up less space.

- You can start your Internet browser from within Instant Accounting. Any browser can be used, though Internet Explorer is recommended by Sage and is essential for interactive support.

- The Sage website has some useful information on its public pages and a great deal more in its SageCover section.

- The Knowledgebase is a valuable source of help on many aspects of Sage software and accountancy.

- The function keys have shortcuts to some common operations.

index